WATER WORKS

Creating a Splash in the Garden

MAUREEN GILMER WITH MICHAEL GLASSMAN

Photographs by Mick Hales

Contemporary Books

Chicago New York San Francisco Lisbon London Madrid Mexico City
Milan New Delhi San Juan Seoul Singapore Sydney Toronto

Library of Congress Cataloging-in-Publication Data

Gilmer, Maureen.
    Water works : creating a splash in the garden / Maureen Gilmer with Michael Glassman ;
photographs by Mick Hales.
        p.   cm.
    ISBN 0-8092-9721-3
    1. Water in landscape architecture.   I. Glassman, Michael.   II. Title.

SB475.8 .G56   2002
714—dc21   2001028838

Contemporary Books

A Division of The **McGraw·Hill** *Companies*

1 2 3 4 5 6 7 8 9 0 SSI/SSI 0 9 8 7 6 5 4 3 2 1

ISBN 0-8092-9721-3

This book was set in Bembo
Printed and bound by Star Standard Industries

Interior design by Kim Bartko
Photographs by Mick Hales
Additional photographs by Maureen Gilmer appear on pages 2, 4–11, 20, 22, 23, 26, 27–29, 31–36,
38, 41, 46, 50, 52–54, 56, 58–61, 63, 69, 71, 72, 74, 77, 78, 81–83, 85, 91, 98–105, 108, 116, 119,
120, 121, 124, 125, 132, 134, 137, 144, 145, 147, 151, 152, 156, 160, 162–164, 166–171, 173, 176,
177, 179, 187, 189–191

McGraw-Hill books are available at special quantity discounts to use as premiums and sales
promotions, or for use in corporate training programs. For more information, please write to the
Director of Special Sales, Professional Publishing, McGraw-Hill, Two Penn Plaza, New York, NY
10121-2298. Or contact your local bookstore.

This book is printed on acid-free paper.

This book is dedicated to
everyone who has dreamed of water in the garden . . .
may their visions become a fluid reality.

CONTENTS

PREFACE

Water Works is a book about you, your home, and your intimate relationship with water. It is about how water functions—specifically, how it works for you in the landscape to solve problems and to enhance difficult environmental challenges. The techniques discussed herein are a collective labor of love that has evolved from ancient designs born out of human need for water in everyday life. All the great cultures have influenced how we see and work with water, and their contributions to the artistic realm of hydraulic engineering have yielded a spectacular heritage of diverse applications over the centuries.

In these chapters, we explore water that works in myriad ways. Some chapters are wholly devoted to the natural waterfall, pool, and streambed to show water's working role in the wild and its realistic adaptations in gardens. We look at how water works to transform our living environment when sculpted in the formal aesthetic setting. We even explore options in easy-to-install self-contained fountains that solve and beautify the most challenging or transient living spaces. Finally, we leap into the depths of pools and spas, where water surrounds the human body and provides visually stimulating opportunities as well as recreational amenity.

Water Works provides a rare overview of the world of water in the contemporary American garden. We explore it with spatial design consideration in terms of use, style, and color. We also review the flood of new products and artwork that transform an ordinary fountain into a miracle of light after dark. We emphasize the role of plants around the water feature rather than focus on those that grow inside it.

Do not confuse *Water Works* with the many books that show how to create a backyard water garden. This is not a book that details water plants and how to take care of them. It is the first in-depth view of the emerging role of water in contemporary gardens, an exploration of how water will prove the most valuable tool for enhancing the human environment of the future. Above all, it is a testimony to the lifetime works of water that speak to us in a primal language that is age-old, proving there is no garden on earth that will ever match that of the new fluid landscape.

ACKNOWLEDGMENTS

We believe all good work is a collaborative effort. Many people helped make this book possible.

Special thanks to our talented editor, Anne Knudsen, and to our dedicated agent, Jeanne Fredericks. We would also like to express our gratitude to the creative ability of designer Kim Bartko, the managing ability of editor Julia Anderson, and the fine copyediting of Jacqueline Blakley.

Michael Glassman wishes to personally thank his wife, Kathleen, and his mother, Elaine, for their support. He professionally thanks Robert Barrow, Rob Littlepage, Ron Stivers, Jennifer Wait, Empire Construction, General Pool Supply, Matsuda's of Sacramento, and Valley Hi Landscape Company.

We also wish to thank the following clients of Michael Glassman, who generously allowed their homes to be photographed and included in this book.

Jim Pastrone and Howard Gray
Linda and Chris Whelan
Erika Akin
Paul and Tenley Coulter
Donald and Mary Ann Ratcliff
Peter Bollinger
Douglas Kay
Sandra Dussault
Mark and Carol Sussman
Joselle Prinzing
Kent and Holly Ramos
Dr. and Mrs. Mark Debruin
Charles and Carla Sigerseth
Donald and Betsy Lyman

He maketh me to lie down by still waters.
—23rd Psalm

Of Human Habitation, Water, *and the* Garden

Buried within every one of us is a primal response to water. It is a living legacy of early humans, who could not survive for long without this precious resource at hand. Water is pervasive in our historic literature; for example, biblical psalms often refer to water as a symbol of life in the dry deserts of the Holy Land. Human beings first settled along natural waterways in the Euphrates Valley, and no camp or village would exist for long without water nearby. While the conscious mind may view water as merely hydration for the body, it is a subconscious reaction that evokes feelings of well-being linked to the very survival of our species.

Design is invariably rooted in the natural world. Water in landscape design, therefore, is the manipulation of natural models to solve problems in the man-made human environment. The natural models provide the foundation upon which the artist, designer, or even engineer may improve on nature in field or landscape.

The most fundamental way to explore natural roles of water in the environment is to separate static conditions from those that are active. Static (passive) water can vary in size from puddle to pond. It can be more intimate, like Thoreau's Walden, or on a larger scale, like Lake Tahoe. The ambient nature of the static condition is one of stillness, producing a mirrorlike surface that reflects surroundings of earth and sky. Though this water does not change a great deal on the surface, the effect may change from minute to minute as weather and the position of the sun alter the reflection.

Animated (active) waters are those that are always moving. No matter how fast or slow, large or small, this ever-changing factor imbues these waters with an almost living character. It is as though the movement speaks to us. Mark Twain wrote that his beloved Mississippi River "told its mind to me without reserve, delivering its most cherished secrets as clearly as if it uttered them with a voice." Many others who have intimately loved rivers and streams believed them to whisper or sing in that wordless language of moving water.

Falling water is perhaps the greatest spectacle on earth, both because of its visual beauty and the sometimes powerful sound. Large waterfalls can be awe-inspiring, which led Africans to name Zimbabwe's Victoria Falls "the smoke that thunders" because of the perpetual mist that surrounds it day and night. Closer to home, Bridal Veil Falls in the Yosemite Valley of California is not famous for its volume, but its height—over 600 feet (183 meters). It falls like a single sparkling thread into the valley below.

Smaller examples prove to be nearly as inspiring, and we are drawn to them inexplicably. Introduce a child to a stream and he will immediately be lured by the waterfalls, or even rapids, where sight and sound touch his primal heart. Build a waterfall in a city plaza and the people will flock to it. We are irresistibly drawn to falling water, whether it is natural or man-made.

Since ancient times, human beings have studied natural models of active and passive waterways. Over aeons we have created them to artificially enhance our daily environment and to bring vital water supplies beyond the shore or riverbank. The first waterways solved problems of agriculture in arid climates by irrigating with ditches that brought river water to dry land. Since that first successful hydrological experiment, people have devised an infinite number of new applications that have greatly improved living conditions and ensured a more reliable food supply.

Water in Nature

Before exploring ways humans have manipulated water to solve problems and enhance their environment, it is important to better understand how water functions in nature. There exist just a few laws that are applied to an infinite number of scenarios.

The botanical term *succession* describes the continual change of the natural environment. No matter how stable it may seem, every ecosystem is in a state of flux. These changes occur so slowly that it is impossible for us to witness them in our limited lifespan.

The simplest example of succession is a natural lake or pond. It begins as a depression filled with water. Over a very long time, organic matter (such as leaves) accumulates in the bottom of the pond, gradually causing the pond to become more and more shallow. Eventually, it will be shallow enough to allow sun to penetrate all the way to the bottom. This fosters a community of aquatic plants or "pond weeds" that grow underwater.

At the same time, reedlike plants called *marginals* colonize the very shallow edges of the pond. The most common example is cattails, which grow with perennial roots underwater, anchored deeply into the muddy bottom.

Their bladelike leaves rise up to grow in the open air. Each winter the cattails die back to become dormant, shedding copious amounts of dead leaves and stems into the water. This further fills the shallow pond until there is little or no water visible at the edges. Over time the edges creep inward toward the center of the pond until there is no visible pool left.

At this stage the pond is reclassified as a marsh, swamp, or bog. This condition is characterized by saturated soil that lacks standing water, except in very wet weather. Bog plants abound in this environment. The marginal plants may remain in the area, but there will be herbaceous plants, such as marsh marigold and pitcher plant, to add beauty and color.

Eventually the site will be colonized by a host of deep-rooted grasses adapted to saturated soil and periodic dry seasons. This precedes the final stage in the succession cycle, a transition from a wet meadow to a dry one. Natural meadows in the wild begin as ponds and grow into the beautiful places we find today.

Understanding succession from pond to dry meadow provides us with the model for our natural water features. Water gardens contain elements of each stage in the succession process, all present at once. We grow aquatic plants, such as water lilies, reeds, aquatic iris, horsetail, and dwarf cattails. We even support bog plants, such as the marsh marigold. At the edges water gardens often feature ornamental grasses, which are the har-

The Grand Canyon is a world-famous example of the erosive force of moving water.

binger of the meadow. There is order to nature, and it gives us a clear picture of how natural plantings in conjunction with water features relate to one another.

Flowing water also experiences its successional changes, although they can be a bit less gradual due to the violence of high water or flood. Rivers and streams everywhere rise with the spring thaw and increased runoff of the rainy season. The power of moving water is vital in sculpting the banks and redirecting the course of the main flow. In the dry months the waterline recedes within its natural banks for a more limited perennial stream. Seasonal, or *ephemeral*, streams, such as those in the desert or in dry climates, may disappear entirely for the season, although there may be flows or pockets of water trapped deep underground.

These seasonal variations govern what grows along banks of rivers and streams. Plants there must not just survive complete inundation in flood times but remain anchored in the face of such flows. They must also adapt to dryness. These plants serve a purpose vital to the survival of the waterway itself. The roots will bind the banks to prevent large-scale erosion and provide shade that reduces the surface evaporation rates in shallow water.

The term *riparian* is used to describe the trees and shrubs that normally live along the banks of streams and rivers. They are vital for the health of the waterway and the survival of related wildlife species.

A mountain stream illustrates how water carves out its path on the land, and the way that plants adapt to its presence.

Trees such as cottonwood shade the water's edge and shelter aquatic reproductive habitat. Shrubs or shrubby trees, such as willow, grow roots in a dense fibrous network capable of binding riverbanks against disintegration in times of high water. Willow branches are made flexible so that they bend, but do not break, under the pressure of fast-moving water. This also provides wildlife important protective cover from predators for safer access to the water. Grasses and sedges act as a green carpet to protect the water's edge from wave and surface action, which can gradually erode sandy beaches.

Each kind of plant in the riparian setting serves a valuable purpose. This multilayered habitat also shows us a model of what kinds of plants belong in our re-creation of a natural stream. None of these riparian plants live in the water permanently, but are inundated with it periodically.

Henry Wadsworth Longfellow tells us in his poem "Keramos" that "Art is the child of Nature; yes, her darling child, in whom we trace the features of the mother's face, her aspect and her attitude." The water-filled landscape created by the hand of a human designer is indeed the child of the natural models of ponds, streams, and all their aspects and attitudes. We cannot envision the child without first knowing the mother; in planning home water landscapes, success is contingent on our understanding of this natural aesthetic vernacular that only nature can provide.

Humans and Water

Water and waterways became different things to different cultures. Many of the great cultures that shaped modern civilization maintained unique relationships with specific waterways. How water was used tells the story of the culture and characterizes the engineering accomplishments of the Western world.

Egypt: A Linear Riverbank Empire

Perhaps the greatest of all civilizations was ancient Egypt, an empire that stretched thousands of miles across a barren desert in twin ribbons flanking the River Nile. It was this single animated waterway that defined the Egyptians, their religion, and their personal vision of the ideal living environment. Egypt is the archetype of all riverbank cultures that relied on that single body of water for travel, power, and food. The Nile itself became the divider of the entire world, separating the realm of the living on the east bank from that of the dead on the west. It was on the side of the setting sun that mummies were embalmed and the sun god Ra descended into night.

The Nile also defined the cycles of life. Before construction of the Aswan Dam in the 20th century, the river spread out over an immense floodplain during the rainy season. This nourished the soil by depositing a rich layer of fertile sediment. After the waters receded, crops were planted and irrigated by ditches carrying water across the newly exposed floodplain from the shrinking river. Without this cycle of flooding it would have been impossible to survive in that enormous desert, much less construct pyramids.

The river was also responsible for the visual beauty of Egyptian art. The lotus plant thrived in the floodplain, its thick fleshy roots anchoring the plants deep in the fertile mud. They would die back to the ground with the dry season while the root lay dormant and insulated from the heat by black river soil. With the flood, lotus came to life again, its leaves and flowers rising magically to stand above the waters. Thus lotus flowers became the universal symbol of resurrection in Egyptian religion, which so thoroughly permeated this culture obsessed with the afterlife.

Perhaps equal to the lotus of Egypt was the papyrus, a reed that dwells in the shallows along the riverbanks. It spreads into extensive, sometimes impenetrable, colonies. Scholars believe it was the papyrus beds that protected infant Moses from the vengeful pharaoh. It was from these auspicious fibrous plants that the first paper was made. In the great temples of Egypt, images of papyrus and lotus appear again and again, painted and carved into the surface of the stone.

The Gift of Hanging Gardens

In the fifth century before the time of Christ, King Nebuchadnezzar of Babylon lived on the fertile floodplain of the Euphrates. His beloved wife, born in the empire of the Persians farther north, grew homesick for the hills of her birthplace. The dilemma facing the king was how to create a mountain on flat land that could be planted in a way that would evoke the forests and waterfalls of the queen's memory.

His gift to her was the Hanging Gardens of Babylon, which became one of the Seven Wonders of the World, although the gardens were already in ruins by the time the Romans described them five centuries later. The legendary gardens covered more than three acres, a pyramidlike earthen structure built with stepped terraces that appeared to hang without support over the surrounding lower levels. The completed work at its highest point reached mountainous proportions, and remained the largest man-made structure in the world until the construction of the Great Pyramid of Giza in Egypt.

The entire construction used the most advanced hydraulic and structural engineering of the day. It was irrigated with a complex system of pumps that pushed Euphrates water upward over 1,000 feet (305 m); the water then flowed downward with gravity through a complex series of wells, pipes, and canals. This system provided cooling waterfalls and supported enormous trees, as well as a wealth of plants and flowers. What was used to satisfy a queen's desires would later become the foundation upon which the Arabs, Romans, and finally the architects of the Renaissance would create their remarkable water works.

Paradise: As Precious as Gold

In the ancient world before the birth of Christ, the eastern Mediterranean was controlled by the empires of the Medes and the Persians, which were far more advanced than the peoples of Europe. They developed the West's early knowledge of engineering, art, literature, and medicine. Much of their empire lay in very dry country from the Holy Land north to the Black Sea. Without a deep understanding of irrigation, people could not cultivate food, much less make their homes comfortable.

Later these cultures would accept Islam; and the Islamic holy book, the Koran, reflected the value of water in a dry climate. The book contains dozens of references to Heaven, described as a paradise garden with rivers flowing out in the four cardinal directions. In fact, patterns on Persian carpets are actually a stylized version of this paradise garden.

Arab architecture closed out the brutal desert landscape and turned its face inward on the precious water source. It was fully enclosed by free-standing walls or by buildings that protected the courtyard and its plants from the drying desert winds. Its form is inspired by the four-quadrant design, which includes canals radiating outward from a central wellhead or fountain. Their challenge was to maximize the experience of water without sacrificing more than was necessary to evaporation.

The Arabs used small jets to shoot thin streams of water into the air. Streams proved less vulnerable to evaporation than spray, and less likely to drift on the wind. Their systems used very narrow, deep channels to transport water with as little area as possible subject to surface evaporation. They devised the multiple-tier fountain, which efficiently concentrates the sight and sound of water falling for its greatest effect on the surrounding space.

As the Arabs swept across Northern Africa and into Spain, the Moors brought with them their walled gardens to cope with the equally arid climate of the Iberian Peninsula. This style then crossed the Pacific Ocean with Spanish explorers into the New World, where it took root in Mexico, then moved northward into California. The California missions would not have been possible if Franciscan missionaries had not used this same aqueduct engineering to bring water to the Southern California desert.

The 18th-century fountain at Mission San Juan Capistrano in California was powered by Old World irrigation systems devised by the Arabs.

The ruins of the baths at Emperor Hadrian's villa outside Rome illustrate the great emphasis on their use in classical Roman civilization.

Roman Ablutions: From Baths to Swimming Pools

The Romans built on the engineering of their Arab predecessors to provide one of the most sophisticated systems in the world. Their aqueducts of brick and mortar carried water for hundreds of miles to feed the city of Rome and other urban centers within their empire. In fact, throughout Rome today are perpetually flowing hydrants of fresh drinking water, the legacy of ancient civil engineering.

What set the Romans apart was their bathing habits. The obsession with bathing and the social milieu associated with communal baths was a vital part of business and daily life. They carried this passion into their conquered territories—the English town of Bath is named for its hot springs and the structures the Romans built to enjoy them in greater comfort. What makes Bath unique is that only the Romans used the facilities, while the natives refused to bathe under any circumstances.

Roman baths were the first interactive water features for health and comfort. The Romans even heated the water in the baths, created steam, and scented the water. It is safe to say that today's spas and steam rooms are the offspring of those early Roman constructions.

Japan: Re-Creating the Essence of Nature

The Japanese garden is perhaps more perfectly modeled on nature than any other landscape. The art of garden making in Japan revolves around the natural laws of flowing water and stone. Over aeons the Japanese have so deeply analyzed nature that the gardens are governed by rigid dictates of arrangement, yet seem random. In fact, creating naturalistic water features such as those of Japanese gardens is far more difficult than any other style.

Japanese garden design has become a treasure trove of ideas for landscapes all over the world. The Japanese designers' understanding of how each stone should sit relative to water and of the way various shapes should be assembled into a waterfall is invaluable to us today. Though this tradition began many centuries ago, it remains just as viable today in the creation of naturalistic swimming pools, waterfalls, and water gardens.

Renaissance Spectacle: Perfection of the Fountain

The Renaissance brought to Europe more than just artistic and intellectual enlightenment. It was a period of great garden making—most important, of making gardens involving water. Combining Arab and Roman engineering, the design of water works for beauty and even environmen-

tal enhancement resulted in matchless water features in the pleasure gardens of Europe.

These landscapes contained virtually every kind of water feature
known at the time. The most incredible of all were those in the hill country, where, like Babylon's hanging gardens, gravity could force water at
incredible pressures into falls and spouts. Among the most magnificent is
the Villa d'Este, in the hill town of Tivoli outside Rome. Not one drop is
recirculated in this water-filled garden, and it operates without a single
pump. This was not a practical creation, but one purely conceived for
human delight and to cool the air of the hot Italian summer.

In the Garden Context

The recurring theme of this book is that the pool or water feature is part
of a larger space or landscape, and thus must be viewed as part of a whole.
Contractors tend to view their work as the priority within a backyard.
Certainly it may be the largest, most visible, or most expensive part—but
you, the user, are the real priority. The water features in your backyard,
both large and small, must contribute to the beauty and comfort of the
overall environment.

The division between
fountain and swimming
pool is often blurred.
This monumental
fountain evolved into a
small swimming pool,
providing maximum
aesthetic impact while
retaining its recreational
role.

No matter how beautiful the water feature may appear, it does not exist
in a vacuum. It exists within the surrounding landscape, which can either
enhance or detract from its visual quality. Therefore the overall space—
the setting and the water feature—must be designed or considered simul-
taneously for all to blend in a seamless and beautiful landscape.

It is plants that give a fountain life, and their soft greenness contrasts
with the stark masonry to create a unique dynamic. Ensure that you may
plant around the new construction by designing spaces that are suitable for
growth. If you will need a tree, save a space where it may grow success-
fully. If there is no drainage in the soil pockets, foliage plants essential to

frame the water feature will die immediately. Consult a landscape architect or
landscape contractor to guarantee that
everyone makes adequate provisions for
planting, drainage, and irrigation of the
surrounding garden.

Water Features and Landscape Design

Every designer is concerned with what the user sees when viewing the
landscape. It may be a specific focal point; or it may be a number of them,
each to be viewed from a different place within the house or yard. The
focal point becomes the pivotal element in a space, and all design decisions
are made with respect to that point.

For a variety of reasons, water features make the best focal points.
First, *they evoke our primal response to water.* We are compulsively drawn to
them as a source of life. Second, *they are animated.* When water is flowing, it is unlike the surroundings of plants or other components, which
are mostly static. Third, *they catch light.* The glistening surface sparkling
in the sunlight is attractive and lends an upbeat, almost festive feeling to
the spaces around them. Fourth, *they sound appealing.* From the tinkle of
spouts to the roar of a waterfall, the sound of water drowns out the rest
of the world.

The fifth reason water makes the best focal point is *pure beauty.* Water
features are beautiful creations that transcend mere brick and mortar,
bringing the world of fine art to any setting. The arrangement of the
feature, its materials, and its juxtaposition to other elements create a composition that is far more dynamic than a mere recreational amenity. It is
this fifth (and perhaps most important) feature that we will stress in this
chapter, because with the costs of building a pool at risk, the final product must be, above all, beautiful.

Today's smaller homes blur the division between indoor and outdoor
living spaces. The indoor spaces must relate directly to those outside, and
the pivotal points governing that relationship are windows and doors.
Even in winter, when you may not spend any time outdoors, a focal point
should still be visually vital to the spaces inside. You see it without necessarily interacting with it. The exception, obviously, is when the feature is
linked to a spa, which is often used outdoors, even in very cold weather.
But in general, this visual connection to the indoor rooms is the foundation that guides where such a feature is best located.

The position of the feature must relate even better to outdoor living
spaces. You will spend a lot of time outside in the warmer months, and the

At left, This beautiful water feature is part of a classic rectangular pool, but it is far from simple. Newly constructed, its design is fully visible; but over time these nuances will be cloaked in a rich vestment of flowering vines and roses. Water is pumped from the pool to the lion's head fountain on the back wall. The remainder of this system—inspired by ancient Arab irrigation—flows by gravity down through various basins and channels into the pool. Top right, The wall fountain has three different pool elevations in its complex system. The first half-bowl is suspended from the wall. It overflows in a perfect ring to the traditional European basin, which is fitted with four smaller spillways featuring granite weirs that sculpt the water into perfect falls. These empty into a large subterranean pool, which is drained on opposing sides by narrow channels. Above, The lion's head fountain is inset into the wall, veneered with marble tiles set on the diagonal. The top edge of the upper basin is carefully capped with pink speckled granite to ensure it overflows with precision accuracy.

Of Human Habitation, Water, and the Garden 15

This beautiful pool and water feature is gently nestled into the slope with careful attention to a gradual rise in elevations from the pool to the walls behind. Such a natural and well-integrated setting can be designed only when the entire site is considered as a whole. When designed without attention to the landscape, the water feature will feel vaguely uncomfortable, and will never reveal its true beauty in the proper context.

water feature should be a focal point of the environment. In fact, many designers optimize this position so that it is seen from as many angles as possible.

Because this kind of water feature is an integral part of a pool, their relationship can be interactive. Pool water features allow you to interact with the water by sitting or swimming under and around the flowing water, rather than just passively viewing the water as you would view a garden fountain. These features provide gathering places that are particularly attractive in very hot weather.

This interactive relationship is personal, which requires the feature to look just as good from 3 feet (about 91 cm) away as it does from 30 feet (about 9 m) away. Attention to detail will ensure its beauty from any angle or distance.

Although the water features of Las Vegas casinos glitter in the sunlight, they literally glow after dark! This emphasizes how vital night lighting can be in setting the nocturnal ambience around the pool. Great lighting tricks enhance the feature so that every ounce of water that flows through is perfectly illuminated. Water feature lighting, coupled with ambient landscape lighting of the surrounding areas, will provide the view from indoor rooms, making the indoors feel like a part of the garden. Success, then, hinges on the position, design, and illumination of the water feature focal point.

No New Ideas

Indeed, there are no new ideas—only the applications of ideas change. Everything has been done, by either nature or the work of human hands. Our human architectural history is a treasure trove of ideas for water features, and throughout this book you will find these ideas adapted to a startling array of new situations.

Although we may live amidst contemporary architecture and suburban lots, the Egyptians, Babylonians, Arabs, Japanese, and the artists of the Renaissance offer us tried-and-true techniques for solving our design problems. The universal nature of water makes it work hard in the hands of human beings. We can use it to thwart the heat, add moisture to a dry climate, delight the eye, and please the ear. It adapts to our needs by drawing wildlife and offering more active recreational amenities.

Let us take a new look at this very old art and put water to work to enhance the ambience of the new American garden. You will learn to view water features not as independent elements, but as just one piece of a much broader scheme. Open your mind to take in all aspects of the environmental landscape so that the whole, that great composition of water and earth and plants, might come together to improve the quality of everyday living at home.

IN ORDER TO COMPREHEND THE BEAUTY OF A JAPANESE GARDEN, IT IS NECESSARY TO UNDERSTAND—OR AT LEAST TO LEARN TO UNDERSTAND—THE BEAUTY OF STONES. NOT OF STONES QUARRIED BY THE HAND OF MAN, BUT OF STONES SHAPED BY NATURE ONLY. UNTIL YOU CAN FEEL, AND KEENLY FEEL, THAT STONES HAVE CHARACTER, THAT STONES HAVE TONES AND VALUES, THE WHOLE ARTISTIC MEANING OF A JAPANESE GARDEN CANNOT BE REVEALED TO YOU.

—LAFCADIO HEARN, *GLIMPSES OF UNFAMILIAR JAPAN*, 1894

STONE, POND, *and* WATERFALL

WATER AND STONE are inseparable in the Japanese garden, just as they are so often paired in nature. The way these two interact touches so many aspects of water garden pool design, even when there is no water in the setting. When you come to understand these vital relationships, you may use stone with confidence, not arranging it arbitrarily but working within a larger scheme. Fortunately, the Japanese garden makers mastered these arts long ago so that we may apply them easily in the traditional, proven ways.

If you spend enough time around mountain streams, you will discover some basic forces that govern how stone and water are organized. Water will always take the path of least resistance, flowing around large stationary objects. Where it pushes into the

bank, the water scours away soil to expose rock, and when the scouring eats away too much bank the slope collapses, sending more hard material into the path of the water. For aeons spring runoff etches new features onto the banks of the river, exposing bedrock or isolating boulders that have been pushed by landslide from rocky outcroppings. It is these boulders that are the defining structure of our artificially created rock water features.

This is the foundation upon which all natural pools and rock waterfalls are made. The challenge is to re-create the serendipitous beauty of nature in a smaller, controlled environment. This process is crucial to the believability of the final creation, for if it is forced or inappropriate, you will sense the artificiality without necessarily recognizing exactly where the problem lies. This is why a natural rock water feature can be at once the simplest, yet the most difficult, to design and build.

The Japanese have made the greatest contribution to our contemporary art of naturalistic water feature creation. In Japan, the ancient art of garden making has been elevated to a near-religious experience. The gardens are rooted in the natural world, with its endless combinations of stone and plant and water. For more than a millennium Japanese gardeners have sought to define this elusive natural beauty and to re-create it in their homes and cities. These qualities do not relate to size but to arrangement, so that a tiny square of ground is considered under the same guidelines as massive lakes and waterfalls.

The Japanese spent centuries establishing a vernacular that makes sense of the apparent chaos of eroding canyons and boulder-strewn riverbeds. They have explored the sizes, shapes, textures, colors, and relationships of stone in the wild so that this beauty may be logically re-created in our gardens.

We have nothing like it in the West, but we may build on this body of knowledge as it guides us through the creative process of designing a natural stone pool and waterfall. Without this understanding, we inevitably succumb to a more arbitrary process of arrangement that is fraught with trial and error.

MOVING ROCK

ROCK IS EXTRAORDINARILY heavy. Creating water features with rock presents a significant challenge because moving large boulders is difficult and potentially dangerous. The boulders must be loaded on trucks, moved to your house, unloaded, and set into position. Getting them positioned accurately takes time, heavy equipment, and experienced contractors. Do not attempt to move very large rocks without the proper assistance and equipment. If you hire someone to do the work, make adequate provisions for moving the rock to its final destination. It is best to hire a reputable contractor who is *well insured* to assist you with this project.

Natural Water: Elusive No More

The art of creating a pond and waterfall is no longer an elusive dream, because new products have made the construction process far easier than it was in the past. Anyone with a vision can create a beautiful natural water feature at home without a great deal of effort or money. A pond and waterfall is one of the greatest ways to improve everyday life because it appeals to us in so many ways. Emotionally, it brings a suggestion of the wilderness into our small personal, and often overly urban, world. The sound of falling water, no matter how faint, is soothing to the soul. The natural beauty of stone and plants at waterside is unmatched by any contrived flower garden.

We take in the visual experience of a rock waterfall and its adjoining pond all at once, in its fully completed form, with all the components made one by means of the water itself. Yet this is actually a composition of various elements, some visible and others invisible. Success comes only when you come to understand the nature of each component, how it is built, and ways that it may vary. You must consider the shell of the pond, its shape and edging, the placement of boulders, and the form of the waterfall. Although working with individual components may be a bit more complex at the outset, the whole project is far more likely to be completed without any major difficulty.

Nuance of Stone

Natural stone is the embodiment of that *vague emotional stimulus* that we as humans experience in the wild. It is a primal reaction that is as difficult to define as the character of stone itself, because no two natural stones are exactly the same. Each will exhibit a difference of color, no matter how slight. Mosses and lichens may change the face of a stone, as will iron stain and weathering. Stone shape is equally as variable—some are rounded smooth as glass by water, while others are chipped by landslides or split by expanding ice. They may be dense and solid, like granite; or porous, like the rough honeycomb of volcanic rock.

The most beautiful stones are those patterned with the patchy hues of minute plants known as mosses and lichen. Their presence will tell you which edges of a boulder are the top and front, because these plants require exposure to air and sunlight to live.

Stone must be carefully chosen for any water feature or garden pool. All the stone should be of the same type and color so that the whole is visually integrated. If stone exists on site, strive to match it. A garden that mixes stone will never appear natural, because in the wild there is not much variation within a particular waterway.

There is also a front and a back, a top and a bottom, to every stone. This choice may seem arbitrary, but if you study boulders in the rock yard you will see a clear difference in color on the bottom of the rock, where it originally sat on the ground. The upper side will have weathered, perhaps showing lichens or other coloration, while the underside may be either pale or stained by the soil itself. Therefore, each boulder will present two clearly different characters, and you must respect each within the context of the water feature. This is why a good waterfall builder will want to handpick stones for the project. Working with stone sight unseen can prove disastrous, resulting in a final product that appears unfinished or ill conceived.

Stone size ranges from that of a pea to monoliths. It is size and arrangement that define the natural waterway. Small stones are prevalent on beaches and in the main flow line of a streambed. Large stones are the chief factor that directs the water to flow in a meandering pattern, and these are the most immediately visible of all. The position of large stones on any water feature must then relate to what the water is doing around them in terms of streambeds, waterfalls, and rapids.

DIVIDING THE STONE

FORTUNATELY, THE Japanese garden makers have given us some classifications that make it easy to evaluate boulders according to their shape. These are divided into five basic types, which are combined with smaller "helping" stones to create a variety of water and garden features. They may represent mountains, hills, canyons, waterfalls, rocky shorelines, pond edging, and beaches. If you become familiar with these forms, it will help you transcend that "vague emotional stimulus" of natural stone. You will begin the personal journey toward understanding the very character of the stone itself. Following are the boulder definitions and their connections in the Japanese design vernacular.

Tall Vertical

This stone is taller than it is wide. It need not be exceptionally tall; the ratio of height to width is the deciding aspect. A tall vertical stone is often used as the taller side of a waterfall, with the base securely anchored in the earth.

Low Vertical

This stone may be as tall as a tall vertical stone, but it is wider. The proportions are more like a true square. It is combined with the taller stone to provide mass in the waterfall.

Arching

This stone is more triangular in shape, set in the ground on one of its points. The shape resembles the number 7, producing a somewhat cantilevered effect. It is used for waterfall edges or to add an irregular character to the water feature. Stones with distinctive veins or striations are popular for this application, and when lacking an arching stone the garden maker will bury a rock of another shape deep in the ground at an angle to create a similar arching character.

Reclining

This stone is roughly representative of a reclining animal. It is used with tall vertical stones to draw the eye more gently to the taller element. It is sometimes considered the same as arching, but merely placed into the setting in a different position or angle of repose.

Flat

There is no mystery behind the shape of this stone, which is among the most useful of all. It may be up to 1 foot (about 30 cm) thick. It is used in the front of a composition,

Standing vertical stones hold the bank so that grasses and moss may grow down to the water's edge in the gaps between them.

or as the central stone around which the other four boulder shapes are arranged. It is a valuable stone for ending paths and walkways by cantilevering over the water's edge. This kind of stone adds a point of access to the pool, and in Japan it was the place where spiritual prayers or offerings were made.

Helping stones must match the stone type of the bigger boulders. They should be of similar color and texture, if not an exact match. They will then fit into your waterfall composition without appearing forced or incongruous. Most features include only three of the five large stone types, with the remainder composed of helping stones.

Pond Shell Requirements

Without question, concrete is important in the construction of pools and waterfalls—it is the fundamental structural material. For visual appeal, the wood-framing studs that support your house are encased in wallboard and siding; in the same way, exposed concrete in a water feature is rarely visually appealing.

You will need to consider some dimensional requirements related to the needs of fish and aquatic plants. Pool depth is gauged by both climate and application. The warmer the climate, the deeper the pond must be to keep water from overheating in the summer. Koi fish require a pool at least 3 feet (about 91 cm) deep, preferably deeper.

The shape of the pool bottom should not be entirely even, but sculpted into steps of varying depths for a more natural appearance. These shelves also provide convenient perches for different water plants, allowing each to sit at its preferred depth. Such shelves also provide a valuable foothold should a child or animal accidentally fall into a deep pond. When inner edges of a pond become slick with inevitable and attractive algae, the step becomes a valuable safety feature.

Many designers consider the shell of a concrete pool as an architectural "sandwich" that is created within an excavation. The overall thickness of the sandwich shell and the number of layers and their constituents vary by climate. Extremely cold northern regions require a different sandwich makeup than those in frost-free climates. Local contractors and landscape architects accustomed to this kind of construction project will know exactly what is required.

HOW MUCH DOES WATER WEIGH?
Most people are surprised to discover that water is actually a very heavy substance. A cubic foot of water weighs 62.4 pounds (about 28 kg); a gallon of water weighs 8 pounds (about 4 kg).

The biggest problem with every pool or water garden is leaking. Besides being a nuisance, leaking can cause water fluctuation that may damage fish and plants. It can also cost a lot of money in water bills to keep a seeping pool full. Remember that the water has to go somewhere . . . and if it's into your neighbor's yard, you may have to pay for the consequences of drowned plants and rotting wood.

Although a pond may not leak at the time of construction, a number of factors can cause leaks over time. The strain of weather extremes and ultraviolet light are brutal on rubber or polyvinyl pond liners. Tunneling rodents will shred liners and create cavities underneath that can tear the liner as the weight of the water bears down on the plastic lacking earth to structurally back it up. A dozen other factors can cause liners and even concrete to fail with time, which is why it's essential to build it right the first time.

Architectural Sandwich Options

Each component of the pool shell makes a different contribution to the overall sandwich. Some are purely structural while others are vital to waterproofing. (The dimensions and sizes given vary with local conditions.)

1. *Sand.* The inside of the excavation is covered with at least 2 inches (about 5 cm) of sand leveled and packed appropriately. This sand will insulate the pond, reduce the effects of soil expansion, and protect the waterproof membrane from damage by rodents or sharp edges of underground rocks.

2. *Rubber liner.* The waterproof layer consists of a 45–60 mm rubber liner, which is the only water-holding layer. It is laid directly on the sand base with edges extending up the walls and well beyond the rim of the excavation.

3. *Mortar-stone liner.* This option uses the same sand and liner base as the first option. Over this is laid a thin layer of mortar as a setting bed. The setting bed then receives a layer of flagstone, which is further mortared into place to produce a natural stone bottom without great expense.

4. *Concrete liner.* Concrete-lined ponds include the full architectural sandwich. This requires that all electrical and plumbing apparatuses be installed before the pond is lined. The sand and rubber liner are installed as in the first option. Then a ⅜-inch (about 1-cm) reinforcing bar is carefully set in a 2-foot (about 61-cm) grid pattern to prevent puncture of the rubber liner.

   The shell of the pond is installed with poured concrete at a uniform thickness of 4 inches (about 10 cm) overall. Concrete must be mixed at a four-sack formula using pea gravel aggregate in a slightly dry mixture, which will allow it to adhere and build up on the sides of the pond. If there is too much water in the concrete, which is the case with a standard formula, it will slough off before it has a chance to set up.

   If the pond is larger than about 10 feet long by 10 feet wide (about 3 meters by 3 meters), then the pressurized gunnite system used in swimming pools yields the best results. This system blows concrete onto the walls and bottom of the pond until it has accumulated to the desired thickness. It is cost effective at this larger scale and allows for better structural integrity.

   Poured concrete is far less porous than gunnite. In fact, gunnite should not be considered a water-holding material, and it will leak if not further sealed. Therefore, after the shell has cured for up to two weeks, apply a final plaster coat as a sealer.

It's easy to see why many people decide to install a swimming pool rather than a very large pond, because at this scale the two constructions are almost the same.

5. *Plaster.* The final inner surface is a thin coat of Portland cement plaster. You can easily add color tinting to this plaster to make it more visually natural, with a dark irregular mottling considered the most realistic choice.

Stone and Pond Edges

Every natural pool, whether or not it features a waterfall, is defined by its edges. If you go out into nature you will find a variety of edge treatments related to how the dry land transitions into the water-filled environment.

This transition can be a gradually sloping beach, which is very difficult to create in a garden setting. It can be a more abrupt drop-off when the shoreline is the natural edge of a rock strata. A cantilevered condition is created when the water eats away at stone or bank, leaving the top layer extending out over the water. This third condition is not common in the wild and is best understood at the edge of a swimming pool, where coping cantilevers out a few inches over the water.

In a well-designed natural pool, the best effects are achieved by combining all three conditions: beach, cliff, and cantilever. Although challenging in small spaces, this can be created with sufficient attention to detail. A Japanese garden master will inspect every inch of shoreline to ensure that no omissions or ill-conceived scenarios exist to spoil the overall beauty of the composition.

One of the biggest threats to naturalistic pools is the improper use of concrete. With its gray-white coloring, concrete stands out sharply against slate or dark iron-stained rock. Concrete does not make a suitable edge material, either, because it will never look like anything but poured concrete. Some have found limited success by tinting concrete and mortar to match their rock colors, but even this can be vaguely disturbing within a natural scene.

Beautifully executed, this concrete-lined fish pond edge is so precisely set that the babytears have crept right up to the waterline. Although some concrete is exposed, it has weathered enough to match the boulder.

It is possible to disguise the concrete edge by topping it with stone. One of the most common applications is to apply flagstone to this concrete base so that the stone edge is cantilevered enough to block the view of the structural concrete shell of the pool. It is important that these stones be securely mortared in place, because the cantilever makes them unstable. Loose stone, particularly where close to areas of foot traffic, can cause accidents and serious liability.

Many homemade water gardens, however, employ loose flagstone edges to cover up the edge of a flexible plastic or rubber pool liner. Cantilevered edges actually shade the upper rim of the liner and increase its lifespan by protecting the plastic from damaging ultraviolet light.

Sometimes you can get away with planting right at the water's edge with plants that drape or cascade. They will cover up the visible concrete, but a thorough cloaking takes time to achieve. Plus, when plants die back or go dormant in the winter, you lose the cloaking effect. For example, matlike *Vinca minor* is a fast-growing cover-up that remains evergreen in reasonably mild climates. Where it is colder, you will have to use a plant such as Boston ivy (*Parthenocissus tricuspidata*) to soften edges.

Boulders also belong in the pool edge because they represent the natural rock drop-off, one of the three edge scenarios we find in the wild. The key here is the word *in*, because they should not sit *on* the water. A realistic boulder setting, whether in a swimming pool or a small water gar-

TOP LEFT, Creeping red fescue is a relative of modern lawn grass that will stay green year-round if watered. Here its luxurious beauty fills in spaces and backs up the stones with wild green carpet. TOP RIGHT, Natural pools can be planted with all the finesse of an English perennial border. All these waterside spaces are cloaked in a visual feast of diverse foliage and flowers. ABOVE, The high-profile marginal aquatic plants grown in the water blend seamlessly into the collection of terrestrial plants on dry land. This composition places far greater emphasis on plants than on water, using that mirrored surface merely as a centerpiece or backdrop.

den, is partially submerged. If you have doubts, simply study photos of beautiful mountain lakes and pools, and you'll discover that virtually all the waterside boulders are located in the water itself.

To achieve this interruption of continuous edge conditions, the rocks must be set within the shell or liner of the pond so that the right water level can be achieved. They are often placed on an intermediate depth shelf that allows for perfect placement in deeper ponds.

This illustrates how important planning is to a successful and realistic pond. The rocks are not set until after the liner, either concrete or membrane, is in place. They must be fully positioned, though, before you can finish the remaining edge. The more interruptions in the edge condition, the easier it is to cover up what concrete edges remain to be addressed with either a pebble beach or cantilever stones.

Though this is but a tiny water garden, it features an excellent assortment of plants that add variety and interest in small spaces. Purple fountain grass, blue-green mondo grass, and a haze of umbrella reeds combine with vibrant red big-leaf cannas.

Staging Falling Water

The waterfall is always the central focus of a natural stone water garden. It is animated and alive, creating sound and movement that turns a static garden into a sensual experience. The degree to which we sense its presence is dictated by its size and its rate of water flow. Some may merely trickle, with water barely visible but the stone clearly present. Or water may flow through in a gushing torrent that is a more powerful presence than the stone structure that surrounds it.

NOTHING IN THE WORLD IS AS SOFT AND YIELDING AS WATER. YET FOR DISSOLVING THE HARD AND INFLEXIBLE, NOTHING CAN SURPASS IT.

—TAO TE CHING

Just as the Japanese have explored the nuances of natural stone, they have also defined the nature and qualities of falling water. They have likened the water flowing through the waterfall to a vigorous and masculine character. The pool into which it flows is decidedly quiet, tranquil, and feminine. The pool is also used as a sounding board to reflect the music of falling water further into the surrounding garden.

Waterfalls can be divided into three basic types defined by the number of falls in the overall composition. *Single-stage waterfalls* will produce just one fall into the main pool below. They are the easiest to build and require the least horizontal space.

Double-stage waterfalls drop to an intermediate pool or shelf, which overflows to fall a second time into the main pool. The shelf or intermediate pool should be to the right or left of the point of origin, but never directly below. This lateral arrangement of the intermediate pool will require more width or horizontal space.

Triple-stage waterfalls require the most horizontal space but need not be particularly tall. The water must flow from the source to the right or left to collect at the first intermediate step. It must then flow from the intermediate step back to the opposite side to the second intermediate step. From the second step it may then fall directly down into the main pool. In general, the triple-stage waterfall is configured in an S shape.

Flesh Out the Setting

Without plants, the waterfall and pool will seem cold, lifeless, and artificial. Remember that wherever there is water in abundance, there will always be plants. Plants associated with waterfalls and natural pond water gardens may be divided into three groups, and these are distributed over the range of environments that exist between dry land and deep water. In

order to choose appropriate plants, you must understand how they relate to one another in the wild.

Plants associated with pools and waterfalls are classified as either *aquatic*, *marginal*, or *terrestrial*. In the wild, each type of vegetation is restricted to a certain part of the pond to which it is best adapted. This creates the order and guides the designer's hand in choosing exactly what will be planted where. It also dictates what you may grow on each of the shallow benches sculpted into the pool wall or bottom.

Aquatic Plants

Aquatic plants include a diverse group that ranges from the ever-popular water lily to some extraordinarily invasive and dangerous water weeds. A true aquatic is actually a plant that lives entirely underwater, and this group includes many popular indoor aquarium plants. They don't survive in outdoor water gardens except in warm, frost-free climates such as south Florida, where many have become a serious nuisance in the wild.

Aquatics are loosely divided into those grown for foliage and those with foliage and flowers. The lesser-known foliage plants, such as parrot feather or water clover, spread out over the water with attractive green leaves. The more easily recognized plants are the water lily and its more tropical relative, the lotus. The flat, round, floating padlike leaves of these plants are decorative all by themselves, but the flowers make them all the more prized. Hybrid water lilies and lotus prefer open, still water and grow best away from waterfalls.

Marginal Plants

Marginal plants are usually reedlike species. Some exceptions are the African tropicals—such as calla and canna lilies—which grow in water just as well as they do on dry land, making them marginals. Plants such as the charming marsh marigold are loosely called *bog plants* and grow in very shallow water or in places where soils are thoroughly saturated but without standing water.

The feature that links all these marginals is their ability to survive on dry land and in the water. They tend to occur in the shallower parts of pools and ponds, while in nature they cling to the water's edge. They are somewhat amphibious, and they don't like water more than about 2 feet (about 61 cm) deep. Marginals tend to develop big colonies—for example, the wild irises that thrive on riverbanks throughout Europe and Asia. In fact, their relatives, such as the Louisiana iris hybrids and Japanese Kempheri hybrids, are standards in water gardens worldwide.

Marginal plants are important to any natural water garden. It is the reedy foliage that visually signals the presence of water in the wild, even if it is a tiny spring. These are valuable in our landscapes because many less–water-loving types can grow in dry land around the pool and waterfall to give the illusion of real marginal plants without the maintenance associated with planting them in the water itself.

Terrestrial Plants

The rest of the plants we will consider for this natural water feature live on dry ground. They are the framework that makes the water garden or waterfall and pool beautiful. This is how you set off the stonework by contrasting it against the green color and foliage textures without any of the concerns associated with water plants. However, it is important to remember the relationships of marginals to water in nature, for this tells you exactly where they belong in your garden.

Planting a Waterfall

The water garden plants we've described fill an entire genera of horticulture, and many excellent books and videos detail their species, varieties, and hybrids. What we don't see is a thorough grounding in the plants that belong around the water feature that are vital to blending its presence into the overall landscape. In fact, too often the water plants are emphasized to the detriment of the overall composition, which must carry the garden year-round.

The Japanese garden again provides us with the perfect model for landscaping natural water features with their rocks and falls. In Japan the gardener strives to achieve a particular idealized vision of nature, and after aeons they have settled on some basic ideas that guide us in landscaping. Remember, they are just guides, not hard-and-fast rules. Let them help you organize the large-scale proportions while exploring the smaller scenarios more intimately.

A Japanese black pine, carefully pruned to this wind-blown shape, creates enclosure and provides tantalizing views of the waterfall behind it.

In Asia, garden makers pay a great deal of attention to preexisting surroundings. They strive for full integration of the new with the old in a
seamless transition. Take advantage of what you already have growing in
the yard to make a gentle, rather than a sudden, transition. If this transition from old to new is too abrupt, your waterfall will appear as though it
was forced into the garden rather than an integral, harmonious part of it.

This approach is equally important in any new water environment,
whether it is a tropical landscape or a wild New England glade. The waterfall is the focal point of a space that may extend far into a backyard or
indoors into the rooms that look out on the water feature. You must never
plant a water feature in isolation, but as part of a holistic scene.

SMALL LANDSCAPES, SMALL LEAVES

TRADITIONAL JAPANESE GARDENS are small, but rich with trees and shrubs that bear diminutive leaves. Black pines, Japanese maples, and azaleas—the backbone species of such gardens—all bear modestly-sized foliage, or what is called a *fine-textured foliage*. Small leaves are in proportion with the small-scale landscape, which is balanced by a pint-sized waterfall, and thus all fit naturally together.

Large leaves will be out of scale and will spoil the balance of the design. If you plan to create a Japanese-style garden, or at least an Asian-inspired one, success hinges on plants that all bear leaves in scale with each other and with the space itself. These are some favorite small-leaf Japanese garden species for contemporary gardens:

It is very important shrubs bear small leaves that can be easily shaped into compact forms.

Botanical Name	Common Name	USDA Climate Zone
Acer palmatum	Japanese maple	5
Azalea hybrids	Hybrid azalea	Varies
Chamaecyparis obtusa 'Nana'	Dwarf hinoki cypress	4
Euonymus japonica 'microphyllus'	Japanese euonymus	5
Juniperus procumbens 'Nana'	Dwarf Japanese garden juniper	4
Ophiopogon japonicus	Mondo grass	6
Nandina domestica	Heavenly bamboo	6
Pinus mugo pumilio	Dwarf mugo pine	2
Sasa pygmaea	Dwarf bamboo	5

The waterfall is the center of the garden, even if it is not in the middle of the landscape. Take time to evaluate how it will be viewed from every point in the house or garden, in winter and in summer. These "windows" should govern your choice of plants. For example, you would not place a large shrub in front of the window, because it would block this important view. Instead, position the shrub to help frame that window and enhance the dimensional beauty of the view. The first step in deciding how to plant your water feature is to determine where these windows will be relative to outdoor living spaces and indoor rooms. These become invisible sight lines that you must preserve whenever possible.

In the traditional style, the Japanese plant evergreens on either flank or "wing" of the waterfall. This creates a more integrated mass, with the

evergreens, usually pines, providing a feeling of hills to ground the barren waterfall's eruption of stone.

We can employ this concept using a variety of materials beside pines for a more varied seasonal experience. Alternatives may be derived from the more cold-hardy needled evergreens, as well as broadleaf evergreen plants that may range in scale from shrubs to bushy trees, depending on whether they are pruned. These will all serve as a valuable background against which more dramatic plants will stand, and they also provide the balance necessary for a more harmonious composition.

Some of the best dense conifers include small-scale species and cultivars from these needled evergreen genera: false cypress (*Chamaecyparis* spp.); larger, upright junipers (*Juniperus* spp.); the beautiful drooping spruce (*Picea* spp.); hemlock (*Tsuga* spp.); and arborvitae (*Thuja* spp.). It is traditional to find broadleaf shrubs such as Japanese holly, *Ilex crenata*, and *Euonymus japonica* in this application.

Call attention to the waterfall itself with a single accent tree that is vivid and bold in as many seasons as possible. In Japan this is often a maple, showy in the fall; or a flowering cherry tree, which blooms in the spring. That tree should be viewed as a part of the waterfall and planted so close to it that both complement each other.

This tree should be an open-headed irregular species that doesn't block views or overpower the waterfall with its mass. The best choice will allow you tantalizing glimpses of the stones and water, or perhaps of vivid green background plants. Over time, careful pruning will shape this single tree into a graceful accent that will draw the eye to the water source flowing beneath its branches. Even more important is night lighting, because you will want careful ambient uplighting in this area so that the tree and water features are gracefully illuminated. Such a view will be enjoyed in every season, whether you're living indoors or out.

Once the flanks or wings are planted and the waterfall accent tree is in place, the next stage is solving problems. Low-growing species are the workhorses of this garden because they cover up unattractive utilities and give the stones a grounded look.

The Plant Groups

These plants should be chosen for their ability to grow low to the ground and produce an abundance of foliage. There are a number of groups to choose from, depending on such conditions as solar exposure and moisture availability.

Group I

Low woodland ferns are important for shaded or partially shaded waterfalls. Sometimes nooks and crannies may be shaded by their surrounding stones. Use small spreading ferns here.

Botanical Name	Common Name	USDA Climate Zone
Adiantum pedatum	American maidenhair	3
Neprolepis cordifolia	Sword fern	9
Pthyrium nipponicum 'Pictum'	Japanese painted fern	3

Group II

Spreading, groundcover-like plants are low-growing and dense. These offer more variety than the ferns because they flower. Buy very young seedlings or plant from flats to take advantage of a rootball that slides easily into slim gaps between the rocks. A single young plant may someday spread over a much larger area, rooting as it travels.

Botanical Name	Common Name	Color	USDA Climate Zone
Ajuga reptans	Carpet bugle	Blue	3
Aurinia saxatilis	Basket of gold	Gold	4
Campanula portenschlagiana	Dalmatian bellflower	Blue	4
Cerastium tomentosum	Snow-in-summer	White	2
Lamium maculatum	Spotted lamium	Variegated	3
Pachysandra terminalis	Japanese pachysandra	White	4
Thymus serphyllum	Creeping thyme	Pink	3
Vinca minor	Dwarf periwinkle	Blue	4

Group III

This group is used to cloak waterfalls without planting pockets or with steep angles where plants cannot grow. If you plant clinging vines and allow them to creep along the face of stones by their own holdfasts, they will travel down through the fissures between rocks. The long runners can also be encouraged to cascade off cantilevered parts of the waterfall. It is essential that these vines be controlled so that they do not completely engulf the waterfall; just a few are capable of rendering a new rock waterfall into an ancient leafy grotto in just a few seasons. Merely clipping them back periodically will direct the new foliage to the places that need it the most.

Botanical Name	Common Name	Color	USDA Climate Zone
Euonymus fortunei 'Coloratus'	Purpleleaf euonymus	Yes	4
Ficus pumila	Creeping fig	Yes	9
Hedera helix	Dwarf English ivy	Yes	5
Hydrangea anomala petiolaris	Climbing hydrangea	No	5
Parthenocissus qinquefolia	Virginia creeper	No	4
Parthenocissus tricuspidata	Boston ivy	No	4

Bright variegated sedges provide excellent contrast against dark stone and deeper-colored foliage plants.

Group IV

The next area of planting encompasses the water edge itself. Here the spreading groundcover plants in the aforementioned groups will effectively cloak the ground plain in a matlike carpet. Lumps of marginals at the waterline break up the shoreline and help to accent the location of rocks on the dry land side. They also soften the edge of the waterfall, where they help to ease the transition from taller rock structures to the waterline, just as the large background evergreens eased the transition from the top of the waterfall to the adjacent landscaping.

Although the marginals have been discussed elsewhere in this book, there are some high-quality choices that are very effective when planted on dry land around the pool and closely nestled into the base of the waterfall. These are large enough to cover up imperfections in the construction, exposed concrete or plastic liner, or a not-so-gracefully-located valve box.

To get a better mental image of what this planting should look like around the waterfall, simply imagine an enormous ball of cotton larger than the waterfall itself. Visualize how the cotton would look if you gently set down the heavy waterfall onto the bed of cotton. The edges of the cotton would puff up as the waterfall further compressed into the cotton. The plants you choose to nestle the whole waterfall, not individual stones, should give that impression when planted around its base. Following are some of the best choices, although dozens of other ornamental grasses will do just as well.

Botanical Name	Common Name	USDA Climate Zone
Carex comans 'Frosty Curls'	'Frosty Curls' New Zealand sedge	7
Cycas revoluta	Sago palm	9
Cyperus alternifolius	Umbrella plant	8
Hakonechloa macra 'Areola'	Golden Japanese forest grass	7
Miscanthus sinensis 'Variegatus'	Variegated maiden grass	5
Pennisetum alopecuroides	Fountain grass	6

Group V

With the accent tree in place and the rockwork nestled into a bed of greenery, the way is paved to add some excitement to the composition. Our focus now is the landscape immediately surrounding the setting. A few well-placed high-profile plants will create an active dynamic that will cement the garden into a well-planned whole. While the accent tree provides the primary focal point, these plants will offer one or more secondary points of attention in their best seasons. Some are included for unique form, others for their texture, and others for their flower color.

Botanical Name	Common Name	USDA Climate Zone
Brugmansia × *candida* Gorgeous pendulous trumpet-shaped flowers	Angel's trumpet	9
Canna hybrids Lush tropical foliage and exotic orchidlike flowers	Canna lily	9
Cornus stolonifera Bright red twigs for super accents in winter	Red twig dogwood	2
Corylus avellana 'Contorta' Twisted, corkscrew growth is oddly unique, in leaf or not	Harry Lauder's walking stick	4
Gunnera manicata Enormous leaves that evoke exotic Amazon jungles	Giant rhubarb	7
Hamamelis × *intermedia* 'Diana' Rare, red ribbonlike petaled flowers in the midst of winter	Diana witch hazel	5
Mahonia japonica Traditional in Japanese tea gardens for fall color	Japanese mahonia	6
Salix caprea 'Kilmarnock' Charming springtime accent and valued cutting material	Weeping pussy willow	6

The front entry walk appears to float over this shallow pool with its beautiful water lilies and rock waterfall. This water is circulated under the house and shared by the chemical-free swimming pool through an ultraviolet filtration system.

ROCK AND WATER
Design by Michael Glassman

EVERY DESIGN PROFESSIONAL has a project that is closest to his heart, that defines him and his ability in a way that few other works can. For Michael Glassman, it is this large, 3-acre (about 12,140-square-meter) homesite on a quiet cul-de-sac in a pricey, oak-tree–covered subdivision. The owners developed the entire property and relied on their designer from the earliest planning stages. This shows great wisdom, for the collaboration of architect and landscape architect always results in a whole project far greater than the sum of its parts.

A LAKE IS THE LANDSCAPE'S MOST BEAUTIFUL AND EXPRESSIVE FEATURE. IT IS EARTH'S EYE, LOOKING INTO WHICH THE BEHOLDER MEASURES THE DEPTH OF HIS OWN NATURE.

—HENRY DAVID THOREAU

The desire was to create a wooded estate that would suggest the hunting lodges of the 19th century, with their rich dark woodwork and surrounding forests. Water would be the essential feature, integrated into virtually every aspect of the property. To create the ultimate in naturalistic landscaping, huge boulders and tons of rock were brought on site. It would be an attempt to re-create the beautiful chaos of nature in a wholly controlled environment.

The owners were fortunate enough to possess another property that was rich in rock, much of it stacked into dry walls by Chinese laborers a century ago. This provided a great source of smaller material, as well as larger pieces. Otherwise, the difficulties of finding such a quantity would have precluded the project.

The overall concept for the site would be drawn from architect Frank Lloyd Wright's famous project "Falling Water," where a house was designed in and around an existing waterfall so that the water flowed underneath unhindered. Michael devised a layout that would develop this concept using an entry pool that flowed under the house and then into the spa and pool in the rear part of the property.

The water used in the front pool, with its water lilies and fish, is shared with the swimming pool. This was feasible because instead of chlorine and chemicals for water quality, a special ultraviolet light system under the house that kills bacteria as the water flows through was installed.

The front entry pond was designed for fish and water plants, and the path to the front door would stretch over the water. This exposed aggregate and brick walk was supported by footings hidden underneath so it appeared to float gracefully.

At curbside you encounter the first hint of the miracles of rock and water in this landscape.

ABOVE LEFT, Building
codes would have
required guard rails on
either side of this walk
if the water had been
over 18 inches (about
46 cm) deep. To bring it
up to this depth, the
pool bottom was lined
with cobbles. ABOVE
RIGHT, This two-tier rock
waterfall illustrates the
concepts of Japanese
waterfall planting, with
the flowering magnolia
accent tree at left, plus
the background wings of
evergreen redwood trees
to provide solid visual
grounding of all the
stone. AT RIGHT, Though
the pool appears simple,
complex engineering at
the edges allows the
boulders to sit below
the waterline.

Such a large body of water concerned the building inspector, who deemed it the equivalent of a swimming pool that would have to comply with all applicable codes and regulations. This demanded that the walkways have railings and the entire area be enclosed with a 4-foot (about 1-m) safety fence, which was unacceptable to both designer and owners. The only way to get around the codes was to make the pool no more than 18 inches (about 46 cm) deep.

The pool was dug deeper than its maximum depth in order to allow for the concrete shell and a layer of Nevada moss flagstones to be layered on the bottom. This gave it a perfectly natural appearance. At such a shallow depth, every inch of the bottom of the pool would be clearly visible, which illustrates

This waterfall is composed of a spa at the middle level that is so naturally tucked into the rockwork you don't notice it right away. This water is circulated out of the pool to the front-yard pond, then under the house, where it is filtered before it falls into the spa and pool via this waterfall.

To preserve the natural
beauty of the oak tree–
covered site, this deck,
which looks onto the
pool and lake, was
designed to protect these
shade-giving trees.

OPPOSITE, Looking down
on the pool and spa
from above, you can see
how water flowing out
from under the house
enters the top pool,
falls into the spa, and
overflows through gaps
in the rockwork to the
swimming pool below.

how crucial such details are when attempting to re-create the natural beauty of
lakes and streams.

The swimming pool was designed after a natural lagoon with a boulder-
strewn edge. The light gray plaster gave the water a rich blue color. It was truly
an engineering triumph, as 75 percent of the pool was on native soil, and the
remainder shares some support from compacted fill. The outer few feet actually
cantilever, which required a tremendous amount of steel reinforcement.

To create such a perfectly natural edge condition, it was essential to notch
the bond beam by creating pockets and shelves along the edge, upon which
the giant boulders were placed. This required a notch to be preconstructed for
every boulder, with the rock set just after the pool was plastered. The largest
boulder exceeded 8 tons (about 7 metric tons) and was placed by a huge
portable crane, then invisibly mortared in place to look as natural as possible.
All of this was essential if the pool was to have partially submerged boulders
without any fear of leakage.

The remainder of this huge site contains many footpaths through woodland
glades beneath the spreading canopies of oaks. At the lowest point a lake was
constructed to lure waterfowl to the site. This is the primary view below the

The deck and
swimming pool look on
the lowest point on the
property, a dam built to
create a natural lake. It
is fed by the circulating
stream on the opposite
bank, which aerates the
water. This is a favorite
haunt of migrating
waterfowl.

decks and pool, fed by yet another waterfall on the far side of the ravine. Creeping red fescue and various lilylike plants are the appropriate species for margins of natural lakes. The forest of graceful deodar cedars (*Cedrus deodora*) makes a fine backdrop for the canyon and effectively screens out the neighbor's properties.

This wood and water landscape is probably not within the budgetary realm of most homeowners. But if taken one piece at a time, it is filled with lessons to learn about how to create with rock what nature does at random. Though the surface may seem simple to create, the reality is that innumerable man-hours were spent in designing and engineering the overall concept, addressing the mechanical challenges of moving large rocks, and hiding this contrivance behind a veneer of careless abandon.

It is the landscapes that extend beyond the realm of typical and reach into the fantastic that inspire wonder in us. This example illustrates that each site and each owner is different, and that, with time and experience, a homeowner's imaginings can take form in a three-dimensional world. A small suburban estate can be transformed into a woodland garden in which the "beholder can indeed measure the depth of his own nature."

The Zen of It All

In the world of Zen, we do not shape the rock but become one with it to understand its most elemental value. Such is true with the rock waterfall; for until we come to accept rock and water on its own terms, we can never create a natural setting that is truly believable. Even the slightest bit of unattractive concrete can ruin a carefully conceived plan.

As makers of gardens, we must accept that each stone is entirely unique, just as is each human being. Whether it exists in a mountain glacial moraine or sits in a rock yard in the city, its intrinsic value is in its individual character. It tells us in the silent aesthetic language of nature that challenges us to discover its essence. For only then will we be able to integrate it into a naturally balanced composition that conveys that final goal of harmony.

I WAS BORN UPON THY BANK, RIVER
MY BLOOD FLOWS IN THY STREAM. . . .
—HENRY DAVID THOREAU, *JOURNALS*, 1906

THE FLOWING STREAMBED

THEY ARE CALLED many names—river, creek, stream—but in all cases, these describe the condition of transient water. The term *transient* refers to the traveling nature of water, which is ever in flux. This differs from a contained pool, which is a permanent and static water feature.

All streambeds are related to drainage and are the result of watershed runoff. They are connected by a hierarchy of conduits similar to the vascular system of the human body. It is a network of arteries leading to the sea. Great arterial rivers are fed by creeks and streams, which are in turn fed by ephemeral drainages that run intermittently—only during the thaw or rainy season.

The dry stream is also an attractive feature that has proved highly valuable in a variety of garden settings. In the western United States, where heat and drought preclude many moisture-loving plants, the natural beauty of the dry rocky mountain or desert drainage has inspired garden makers. Because dry streams naturally occur as a depressed drainage feature in the wild, they are often integrated into drainage swales of the landscape or created for their natural beauty alone.

The dry streambed or waterless feature has also been integrated into traditional Japanese garden designs. Light-colored sand or fine gravel is used in lieu of water, and special rakes are used to create an ever-changing surface pattern that undulates just like a real flowing stream. They carry out the design of water in nature so effectively that these gardens include islands and bridges that span the gravel to further support the illusion.

This kind of landscape also provides the foundation for stylized wild gardens designed to capture the luxury of nature without the burden of a water garden. In arid regions it is not uncommon to find basins set into the ground within this dry streambed to lure birds and other wildlife into the garden for a drink. This is a whole garden within itself, featuring wildflowers, nectar plants, and a host of natives that prefer a drier existence.

Dynamic of Flowing Water

Before discussing applications, it is helpful to understand how water influences the appearance of a streambed. Water is the most powerful land-sculpting mechanism on earth. When moving across land, it produces a natural scouring action that picks up particles of soil and carries them away in suspension. This is why rivers are often muddy-colored when in flood stage.

WATER, WHETHER IN OOZING CURRENTS OR PASSIONATE TORRENTS, DISCRIMINATES BOTH IN THE SIZE AND SHAPE OF THE MATERIAL IT CARRIES.

—JOHN MUIR, *OUR NATIONAL PARKS*, 1901

The speed or velocity of water is the deciding factor in the sculpting process. The faster water flows, the more it whips up small particles into solution, and the greater its strength to move larger, heavier pebbles. This movement of earth by water is called *erosion*.

Farther downstream, the flow of the water slows down, perhaps when encountering a bank. When the water slows down, gravity causes the suspended particles to drop out. The accumulation of these particles is called *sedimentation*. Whenever there is erosion, there will be an equal amount of sediment deposited somewhere downstream.

In most streams the flow line, or center, snakes back and forth to undercut the bank on one side and create a beach at the opposite turn. The particles eroded from the cut bank naturally drop out as water slows to make the next turn. Erosion and sediment, cut bank, and beach undulate in a natural rhythm that is the way of water everywhere. You may never have realized that there is a certain logic to the position of beaches on riverbanks. But these rules of erosion and sedimentation are your guide to the logical architecture of a realistic streambed, wet or dry. You must always visualize it as a flowing stream in order to know how to arrange the rock and gravel into a realistic composition.

Understanding River Rock Placement

The stones found in riverbeds and at the seashore vary greatly from those found in fields or in the mountains. These river rocks have existed in fast-moving water where millennia of tumbling has worked them into more efficient, rounded forms. These will vary in size, from enormous river-worn boulders to tiny rounded pebbles. They all share one feature: a pronounced lack of sharp edges.

If you look into the water of a natural streambank, you will see that the stones there vary in color. There will be white and brown, some red,

In this re-creation of
a dry streambed, you
can see the rounded
shapes of cobbles and
gravel that belong in a
flowing streambed.
The gradation of sizes
shows you the likely
path of least resistance
that the water would
follow.

black, and occasionally green, depending on what
kinds of strata the river cut through upstream.
Unlike the uniformity of boulders in the riverbed,
gravel is far more transient and thus diverse. This
illustrates why using river-run gravel for the dry
streambed is far more desirable than crushed
quarry gravel that is of uniform color.

Mountain streams contain a variety of rock
sizes, and it's not uncommon to find that the water
has separated much of it into locations of similar-
sized material. Small pebbles are most common on
the beaches, where they were deposited by high,
fast-moving water. They may also occur at the
deepest points of the river, where gravel accumulates unaffected by surface flow.

You will find that alignment of the stream
responds to the presence of boulders that force the
water to snake around them. These are the pivotal
stones of your streambed, too, and they define
where the theoretical centerline is located.

Use these concepts based on natural models as
your guide. They can be applied in a step-by-step
process that is far easier to achieve in the field than
it is on paper. In fact, landscape architects know
that a design they lay out on paper is only concep-
tual, and the success of the project is dependent on
a practiced eye in the field. You may have a loose sketch as a guide, but the
real art of it will occur in the field. Take your time and study each of the
following steps while continually visualizing where the centerline of the
flow will occur. Strive to keep that flow line identifiable, for that is the key
feature that separates a streambed from an ordinary rock garden.

1. *Set the pivotal boulders.* Position these large stones to reflect your
   proposed alignment. You should know in what direction the
   hypothetical water is flowing. Remember that a snakelike S
   form, no matter how slight, is always preferable to a straight line.

2. *Decide where the water will cut the bank.* These positions will be
   relative to the pivotal boulder. The water flows around the boulder and then into the opposing bank, which it will gradually
   erode until encountering bedrock. Use larger flat stones here to
   define the edge of this bank with a slight cantilever or sharp
   edge.

3. *Use the banks to establish the position of beaches.* The water hits the
   bank and is forced to turn and deposit the beach on the oppo-

site bank. Use smaller pebbles to create a beachlike effect here.

4. *Fill in the flow line.* Use the smallest pebbles in the center, then distribute progressively larger pebbles as you fan out toward the banks.

A variation on this four-step process may include an island created within Step 1. The island will need a larger boulder as an anchor stone, and its surface should lie at the same elevation as that of the adjacent banks. This is only logical, because if water was in fact in the riverbed the island should be elevated enough to naturally remain dry. To achieve this elevation without consuming too much space, you will need steep stone banks to define its limits.

The riverbed should be slightly wider to accommodate the island, because in nature the center flow line of the stream will split in two, go around the island, then return to a single flow on the other side. Islands can also be planted with a bonsai tree or a similar focal plant to further indicate it is not an underwater feature but a green and growing one. The island can be a valuable asset when creating bridges in order to break the single long span into two shorter, more manageable ones.

There are some other features that you may wish to integrate into your dry streambed that will depend on its size and location. If there is a point at which your walk or path crosses over the bed, you can integrate two different features inspired by Japanese applications.

In the traditional Japanese garden, these precisely created stepping stones cross over a much deeper water-filled channel.

Stones in the Stream

The simplest application is to position stepping stones in the streambed, with each treated as its own little island. These should be large enough for a foot to step on and must contain sufficient flat surface at the top to make them safe to cross. This is not a bridge; if water were there, it would flow between the stones themselves.

Bridge

The second method for crossing is a bridge. In American gardens this feature is too often poorly done, appearing to be an afterthought or just ill conceived. It should *not* look like a miniature golf course, but consist of a more natural crossing. Japanese garden makers use a variety of natural

This stream is crossed by a great moon bridge, which is not a realistic possibility for most landscapes. The white granite bridge in the foreground uses a single island in the middle that provides the support for two separate slabs. This simplifies spanning water features without the advanced structural requirements of long bridges.

Stone slabs, though incredibly heavy, are the ideal bridge material because they are very strong and do not deteriorate with time.

materials, such as large slabs of stone, old timbers, and bamboo slat bridges. In order to expand the options, many Japanese riverbed crossings are supported halfway across by a single narrow standing stone anchored in the streambed. This allows you to use two smaller bridges rather than the challenging single-span bridge, opening the door to use many more creative materials.

You can easily copy the Japanese style by using tinted and textured cast concrete slabs, large flagstones, salvaged wood, or bamboo. Make a concerted effort not to choose the European-style bridge, as it will spoil the natural beauty of the streambed and produce an incongruous element or color. Avoid paints and vivid wood stains. Strive for as natural and weathered an appearance as possible.

Japanese Water Basin

You may be surprised to find out that Japanese gardeners actually include water basins inside their dry streambed. This is a common scenario in the dry tea garden, with the ritual water basin set onto the gravel as a symbolic feature. The stoneware ceramic basin is coordinated with the natural earthtone color of the surrounding bed or banks. Although the basins in Japan are for tea ceremonies, in the West they have proved an ideal means of drawing birds into the streambed itself.

Planting Naturally with Grasses

The dry streambed in the wild supports plants that are naturally able to cope with extremes. They must stand up to high-velocity flows of water during the wet season and remain alive during the dry. In the Western deserts and drier prairie regions, the cottonwoods are often the only trees that grow along these drainages. Their roots are strong and venture down to access moisture trapped deep underground during drought.

The only other kinds of plants naturally adapted here are grasses and sedges, which cloak the banks to hold the soil with a network of fibrous roots. Sometimes willows also occur, but they are not as tolerant of the dry season and therefore are rarely found in totally dry riverbeds.

The grasses are perhaps the most populous group of plants on earth, and can be found on all continents except in the Arctic. They range in size from ground-hugging tundra grasses to mammoth Sudan grass of Africa. Garden makers have only recently come to appreciate the unique forms, creative textures, and subtle colors that make the more ornamental species ideal accents in the dry landscape. It is probably the graceful flowing character of the grasses that is so appealing, because a slight breeze creates a fluid movement resembling that of water.

There are many grasses to choose from, but a handful of stellar performers dominate the market. Some are very cold-hardy, while others less so are unique in coloring. Grasses are valuable tools for making boulders look more settled into the site. Because they lack woody parts, grasses are easy to plant, and they adapt to spaces between stones without dislodging them. Best of all, they thrive with the resilience of wayside weeds in what can be a dry, otherwise forbidding landscape.

Fountain Grass

Named for its graceful fountainlike shape, this rather tender perennial grass was the first to gain widespread acceptance in today's market. It

STREAMBED WEED CONTROL

YOU CAN REDUCE future maintenance on the streambed by using weed-blocking landscape fabric during the construction process. It should be laid out to cover all the soil surface after grading but before placing the stone. Set both boulders and gravel directly on top of the fabric. Although the fabric won't last forever, it is important to preventing existing weed seeds in the soil from sprouting. It's also good for preventing new seed blown in from sprouting, but any that do sprout may be easily pulled out because their roots are too shallow to take hold. If you want to add some plants to the finished streambed, simply cut holes in the fabric and plant through it for best results.

matures and flowers so quickly that some of the more dramatic colored hybrids are planted as annuals in climates beyond their hardiness zone. Big, vigorous plants are remarkably drought tolerant and are often grown alongside Western natives and wildflowers.

Botanical Name	Common Name	Qualities	USDA Climate Zone
Pennisetum alopecuroides	Fountain grass	Most hardy	6
Pennisetum setaceum	Fountain grass	Rugged	9
Pennisetum setaceum 'Rubrum'	Purple fountain grass	Very showy	9
Pennisetum 'Burgundy Giant'	Burgundy giant fountain grass	Often grown as dramatic annual	10

Maiden Grass

Cold-hardiness has made this enormous group the favorite of temperate zone gardens. Big, vigorous plants make a strong statement, with many showy cultivars. This may be too large for small-space gardens, as some may reach 7 feet (about 2 m) tall when in bloom. It is ideal for natural landscaping for accent or background on larger sites.

Botanical Name	Description	USDA Climate Zone
Miscanthus sinensis 'Gracillimus'	Best known cultivar	5
Miscanthus sinensis 'Variegatus'	Variegated Japanese silver grass	5

Blue Fescue

This is the smallest of the ornamental grasses, but its coloring yields a very strong presence. It is often grown in clusters or groundcover-like stands to soften the hard stone surfaces in dry streambeds. This grass is loved for its amethyst silver-blue foliage and delightful blond flower spikes. It is popular among cutting-edge contemporary designers who appreciate its qualities in the minimalist modern landscape. There are a dozen or more cultivars, but the following are recommended.

Botanical Name	Common Name	Height
Festuca glauca 'Elijah Blue'	Elijah blue fescue	8" (20 cm)
Festuca glauca 'Blausibler'	Blausibler blue fescue	6" (15 cm)

A DRY RIVER RUNS THROUGH IT
Design by Susan Elmore

WHEN THE DRY streambed is well designed and planted, there results a garden of singular beauty. It is a place where textures take center stage while colors are naturally subtle and muted. It is a garden that comes alive as breezes ruffle the blades and flowers of the grasses, providing through them a feeling of water that was never there.

IN THE PLACING OF STONES FORMING THE ROCK GARDEN, VALUABLE LESSONS MAY BE GAINED FROM A STUDY OF NATURE. NOT THAT WE WANT TO IMITATE NATURAL FEATURES OR ERECT A MINIATURE ALPS IN A SMALL GARDEN, BUT BECAUSE NATURE'S ARRANGEMENT OF ROCKS IS NEARLY ALWAYS BEST SUITED TO THE GROWTH OF PLANTS.

—CHARLES THONGER, *ROCK & WATER GARDENS*, 1919

This soft and flowing landscape is an example of how two schools of streambed planting can be combined into one garden. It is rooted in part in the small-stature perennials found in the alpine style of rock gardens. An abundance of fabulous ornamental grasses have been planted, with each allowed to stand on its own as a statuesque vignette of the tallgrass prairie.

All the best qualities of the dry streambed landscape are combined here to reduce water consumption without sacrificing natural beauty. The entry features the Japanese garden technique of bridging water with large stepping stones. It is no small feat finding nice-sized flat-topped stones such as these, and even more difficult to place each so that it gradually rises to meet the finish elevation of the front porch deck surface.

The entry stones pass over part of the dry streambed that winds through most of the garden and helps to drain it during the rainy season. It is created with stone perfectly matched in tone and character. The otherwise level ground plain has been gently graded to provide a distinct flow line, which also functions to keep the whole landscape well drained. The flow line is also flat enough to double as a convenient trail or pathway to access the rear of the site.

The excavated soil was used to raise the adjacent planting areas above the surrounding grade for improved drainage without importing topsoil fill. A different kind of stone, this one with unique patterns of moss and lichen, was planted into the earth at key points in the design. These provide natural outcroppings that make the elevated areas appear more logical in the overall setting. The boulders also provide an important point of reference around which the plants are arranged.

ABOVE LEFT, This home's
entry is paved with
enormous stones in a
gravel field. The stones
pass over the dry
streambed, which lies
just before the front
porch. ABOVE RIGHT, As
the ground plain dips,
the stones are raised
proportionately higher,
bringing the pedestrian
up to the elevated wood
deck. AT RIGHT, The
architecture of a natural
stream is illustrated
here sans water. Note
that boulder and beach
alternate, just as they
would in nature.

Among the smaller plants found in the streambed are the blue fescue (*Festuca ovina glauca*) and common thrift (*Armeria meritima*). There are also soft lavendercotton (*Santolina chamaecyparissus*) and sand verbena. On a larger level are tall maiden grass (*Miscanthus sinensis*), tufted hair grass (*Deschampsia cespitosa*), and the fluffy heads of Mexican feather grass (*Nassella tenuissima*). As the season progresses, all these grasses will gradually take on beautiful gold and russet tones in the fall.

This landscape is an excellent example of how the dry streambed in an arid garden setting can not only be beautiful, but solve problems as well. A poorly drained site can be made to gently shed into the central streambed, which will shunt runoff and keep the planting areas well above saturated soil. It also shows how a rather uninteresting entry can be transformed into a transitional experience through the ancient Japanese technique of bridging a suggestion of water and thus reinforcing the illusion.

Everything in this landscape is important, from the mounds of mugo pine to the smallest wildflowers creeping through the pebbles. It gains its greatest qualities through grasses, which until recently were considered nothing but enormous weeds. In the painter's eye it has become a living palette of plants and stone naturally combined with a soft and free hand to create something supernatural out of a humble drainage swale.

ABOVE LEFT, Instead of a formal path within this wild garden, the flat bottom of the dry streambed provides convenient access to this fenced kitchen garden at the rear of the property. Note the animation of the tall grasses as the wind ruffles the flowering heads. ABOVE RIGHT, The plants around this house are a palette of unique colors and textures. In this small setting are blue fescue in bloom, and at the rear a stand of horsetail reeds are growing in a tiny water-filled hole amidst the boulders.

Planting Inspiration from Alpine Gardens

If you were to climb the higher elevations of any mountain range, you would pass the tree line into a landscape open to the sun and elements. Trees may exist, but are stunted by snow and wind into gnarled forms that inspired the art of bonsai. Elsewhere, the landscape is composed of rocky cliffs that provide the habitat for a host of rugged plants that thrive under these brutal conditions.

What makes alpine plants able to grow so well in such an inhospitable environment? It is a large tap root that ventures well into fissures in the rock and down deep to find soil moisture far below. However dry it may appear on the surface, the plants are thriving on accumulated moisture trapped under the rock.

These plants all evolved with relatively short stature. This keeps the leaves close to the ground, where they are protected from the cold, dry alpine winds. They leaf out quickly at the close of the spring to flourish and flower before the first early cold of autumn.

Many valiant attempts at creating this kind of garden have resulted in dismal failure. The chief reason is that although plants appear to be growing *on* rocks, they are actually growing in the deep soil *between* them. A small depression is insufficient to support plant life, particularly in a hot climate when the stone itself can absorb an incredible amount of heat. The key is to create deep root zone pockets when setting the stone, and then to water the plants in a way that guarantees this zone a thorough soaking.

Alpine conditions and the rock gardens modeled after them offer us a beautiful and colorful way to plant the edges of dry streambeds. Tucked

between rocks and boulders, these rugged small plants can be far more beautiful than the traditional riverside plant palette. Not all plants need be alpines, as long as the plants chosen share the same needs.

This concept can be used to plant dry streambeds with native wild-flowers, such as Texas bluebonnet, California poppy, mariposa lily, and a host of shortgrass prairie species. These may be planted as seedlings if perennial, or grown from seed sown directly into the streambed provided there is no weed-blocking fabric underneath to prevent root development.

Explore these groups of willing small-stature perennials that will make dry landscapes a beautiful garden. Some genera include a diversity of species and cultivars that represent nearly every climate zone, so it is best to explore those most widely grown in your immediate region.

Once planted, there is no sign of the rock unless you go very close to see it peeking out between the plants. Those cloaking the upper levels are more typical of alpines, which must grow low to the ground to stay out of the wind and avoid snow damage. Around the pool below, more luxurious seasonal plants abound in the moisture.

Botanical Name	Common Name
Anemone sylvestris	Snowdrop windflower
Armeria meritima	Thrift
Aubretia deltoides	Aubretia
Aurinia saxatile	Basket of gold
Erica × darleyensis hybrids	Heath
Festuca glauca	Blue fescue
Geranium cinereum	Cranesbill hybrids
Iberis sempervirens	Candytuft
Iris pumila	Miniature bearded iris
Phlox subalta	Creeping phlox hybrids

THE EVOLUTION OF HABITAT
Design by Michael Glassman

EARLY IN HIS career, Michael Glassman began a project that would continue
for a decade. It was a featureless city lot, and his aim was to create a habitat
for the owner's collection of beautiful waterbirds such as wood ducks. Making
habitat on a flat and barren site was no small task.

THE WATER IS THE ELDEST DAUGHTER OF THE CREATION, THE ELEMENT UPON WHICH THE SPIRIT
OF GOD DID FIRST MOVE, THE ELEMENT WHICH GOD COMMANDED TO BRING FORTH LIVING
CREATURES ABUNDANTLY. . . .

—IZAAK WALTON, *THE COMPLEAT ANGLER*, 1653

The site was divided into a few main spaces. At the rear of the house was a
wood dining patio deck. On the far end of the lot was an enormous koi pond
with a central island that would provide the ducks with a safe haven protected
by the moat of water from marauding domestic felines. At the far end a

AT LEFT, The skill of the designer is indisputable when you consider that this site was nothing more than a bare, flat wall
surrounded by a board fence. AT RIGHT, In the newly completed landscape, the gazebo stands out as the most prominent
element. The water and rocks enjoy no shade, so all areas require sun-loving plants.

waterfall would provide a more distant focal point that filled the entire site with the sound of falling water. A meandering streamlike waterway connected the patio to the koi pond, and a walk over a stone bridge led to a wood gazebo central to the habitat area. This structure allowed close-up viewing of the pond and its wildlife in every season or weather condition.

The earth excavated out of the pond area was gently mounded to create berms on two sides of the pool so that it appeared to be pressed into the

ABOVE LEFT, Looking back toward the house from the central gazebo, you can see how carefully the rocks are arranged in the streambed. The bridge is cast concrete topped with slate to match the patio. This garden becomes a vital oasis for outdoor living in a climate where temperatures can exceed 100 degrees for weeks at a time. ABOVE RIGHT, The main koi pond is now so well shaded that the wood ducks enjoy a great variation in habitat conditions. Their wings have been clipped to keep them at home, and the island in the center of the pond provides a vital protective haven from prowling neighborhood cats.

ground. Berms also elevated the base of all the surrounding screening plants for better separation from neighbors on every side. The open site had to be shaded, and over time a circular grove of California redwood trees matured to enclose the pond, transforming it into a private wildlife sanctuary.

Today the site is cool and shady during the hot California summers. The old wood deck was replaced by a lovely multicolored Indian slate patio. Planting was changed, as well, to better adapt to the now shaded conditions. More naturalistic ornamental grasses and sedges that have only recently come into the landscaping market were added. The garden also features dwarf woodland iris and shade-loving ferns. It is a landscape forever in transition, just as nature is never static but changes and evolves over time.

Return to Nature

Natural gardens that rely on stone to create singular beauty are at once the simplest and the most complex to create. No architect can define the exact nature of a stone, sight unseen. It is the hand of the contractor that will ultimately design the stream in the field and arrange each pebble. And planting cannot be located with certainty until the stones are firmly in their final positions. When nature is the model we seek, there is no way to force our ideas on the site and expect them to be beautiful.

The garden must be conceived in three dimensions, and the designer must visualize the end result when plants and trees are fully mature. Such vision is rare and requires a great deal of experience to conjure. Hence we find the greatest challenge of all gardens: the reality that they will be forever in a state of flux. Unlike buildings, which remain the same, the landscape is an evolving habitat that asserts itself gradually, one season at a time. Then we discover, rather suddenly one day, that the garden has matured, and nature is no longer just the model . . . it is re-created.

WATER WAS A PRIME ELEMENT IN ARCHITECTURE, HERE AS IN ROME, AN ELEMENT TO
BE GIVEN SHAPE, FORM, LIKE OTHER MATERIALS, SUBJECT TO CONCEPTION AS
VARIED—LEFT FLAT AND STILL OR USED IN OTHER SIMPLE WAYS ON OCCASION, BUT
MORE ELABORATE IN ITS FACES AND KINDS OF MOTION. IT IS THE ELEMENT OF
DISTANCE, AND THE UNDEFINABLE CO-MEDIUM OF LIGHT. . . .

—ELEANOR CLARK, *HADRIAN'S VILLA*, 1974

DESIGN *and the* FORMAL FOUNTAIN

WHEN IT COMES TO fountains, all roads lead to Rome. Sure, there were monumental water works in Babylon and Egypt, but it was the Roman Empire that elevated engineering and design to the level we know today. The empire originated in the arid climate of Italy, with long, hot summers in which every drop of water was precious. This forced economy led Roman engineers to build precision aqueducts that carried water many miles across the dry land to supply their cities and villas. Many of the aqueducts still stand two millennia later, attesting to the builders' skill. In Rome, this legacy is a working portable water system that provides public drinking spouts and fills fountains throughout the city today.

This is one of the many public spigots in Rome that produces an unceasing flow of cool, fresh drinking water through a living vestige of the empire's extensive system of aqueducts.

All Roads Lead to Rome

Until the aqueducts were built, each Roman house contained an underground cistern that collected and stored rainwater. Most residents resorted to wells if groundwater was shallow enough; some were forced to draw water from rivers and springs, which limited where they could live. Villas, towns, and other settlements were built at a lower elevation than the spring or river so that a gravity-fed system could pipe water into the homes. The supply of the water source strictly dictated the overall size of the settlement.

Because water was vital to everyday life, the more upscale residents piped spring water directly into their homes through pipes made of lead, terra-cotta, or wood. The architecture of that day arranged rooms and porticoes around a central courtyard, and the basin created there to hold the household water was also highly visible. To keep the water pure, the basin required circulating water—but without pumps, this demanded a flow-through system. When the basin was full it overflowed into a ditch to irrigate plants of the *hortus*, or gardens, downstream.

Although effective, this system was not efficient. In cities like Pompeii, the homes did not have their own water source. Instead, the city built flow-through fountains at regular intervals in the city streets for the residents to draw from. With a hilltop layout, a single system could flow through dozens of communal basins on its path through the city.

The Roman fountain builders understood the concept of head pressure, which meant that water flowing downhill through closed pipes gained a certain amount of pressure. This pressure could force the water at the lowest point upward through a stand pipe. Their general design rule was that water can only be made to rise as high as its source. Thus, water would have to fall 3 feet (about 91 cm) over any given distance of pipe to feed a fountain that was elevated less than 3 feet above the supply source.

The wealthy Romans used this concept to artificially feed fountain spouts in their courtyards, but it was a laborious system that depended on a number of slaves. This method necessitated a water tank on the roof of the Roman house at the highest point possible. This maximized gravity pressure at the fountain basin below. Slaves drew buckets of water, hoisted them to the roof, and filled the tank. Once the tank was full, a valve could be opened to allow water to flow down and into the fountain, and then head pressure pushed it upward to the spout.

ART AND WATER

FOUNTAIN DESIGN CAN be classified in two ways. First are the designs in which the structure or sculptural elements are dominant; this type has been the most common since the Renaissance. Their distinguishing quality is that they remain artistically interesting even when not in operation. The second category includes those designs in which the water itself is the primary feature. These are characterized by jets and sprays that originate in a pool of water. When the water is not flowing, there is little to see except the glassy surface of the pool.

This bronze cherub fountain is an example of the sculpturally dominant fountain, which is attractive whether operating or not.

If a special event in the home was planned, the tank would be filled ahead of time. The valve was not opened until guests arrived, but supply rarely lasted more than two hours before the tank required refilling. Because of the short period of operation and the requirement of powerful slaves, these early fountains in Roman homes became an outward expression of wealth and status.

We learn from this scenario why design of very early fountains, and those of dry Islamic and Persian gardens, used thin jets of water. If the source had to be filled by hand, it proved far more efficient to use a highly visible pencil-thin jet of water more resistant to evaporation. More important, the low volume of this thin jet required less pressure to operate. This, in turn, extended the time the fountain could operate before refilling the tank was necessary. Jets proved to be a design feature born from the hydrological limitations of the ancient head-pressure–based systems.

When aqueducts became more prevalent in Rome, residents could enjoy a continuous supply of piped water under increased pressure. The benefits of gravity flow and accumulated head pressure on miles of aqueduct pressurized the city pipes, which were more accessible to less wealthy households. The ruins of many pools and fountains amidst the emperors' palaces on the Palatine Hill overlooking the Forum attest to the abilities of these pressurized water systems. The expansive water features on the Palatine exist nearly 100 feet (about 30 m) above the surrounding city.

After a long period of decline following the end of the empire, the Roman aqueducts were restored in the 16th century. In the process, the city developed a series of elaborate municipal fountains. These improvements in hydraulic engineering, combined with the explosion of art in the Renaissance, yielded designs with massive sculptures, multiple spouts, and a variety of special features that would lay the foundation for our modern water works.

Dissecting the Fountain

What began as a functional means of ensuring water quality in the Roman house gradually became an art form itself. Despite a diversity of applications, most fountains can be dissected into two main components: the source of the water and the receiver of the water, or basin. It is safe to say that all fountains are essentially no more than an adaptation of this fundamental source–recipient relationship.

The beautiful carved stone urns so loved as decoration for Roman homes found their way into the household fountains as an aesthetically interesting water source. The urn was placed at the center of the preexisting basin or open cistern of the household. The center of the pedestal base was drilled out so that water could be forced up from a pipe underneath. The urn filled with water and then overflowed into the basin below.

The Romans discovered that if the rim of the urn was beaded or scalloped, the water flowed out in channels rather than in a sheet. This made the stem of the urn more visible; so eventually the decoration on these stems grew progressively more elaborate, often depicting leaves and stems of plants. The design of these Roman fountains and their surroundings was preserved for history in the time capsule of Pompeii, where excavations have exposed frescoes that depict such fountains and their gardenesque surroundings.

It was this simple urn design that grew increasingly complex until the fountains featured two, three, and even four sequential bowls in a single tower. At the top, spouts were disguised by decorative figures in bronze or elaborately carved stone dolphins, birds, and snakes. The pinecone was a very popular motif because those of the Italian stone pine (*Pinus pinea*) were a Roman symbol of fertility and rebirth. Pinecone fountainheads were perforated in many places to allow water to flow down all sides into a bowl, compared to the single spout of the animal motif.

Fountains later became integrated into sculpture that stood at the center of a bowl, water issuing from somewhere at the top of the figure. Human forms were carved to carry a water jar or urn, out of which the water would flow. The most common figure is called the *putto*—a pudgy

child shouldering a large jar. Animals were also used, the water flowing out of the mouth.

When space was a problem, which was often the case in densely populated Rome, a different kind of fountain called a *fluvial outlet* proved more efficient. Rather than the urn and bowl standing alone as a central element, this type of water fountain was pushed up against a wall.

The spout was disguised behind a carved stone face that represented a river god with wild eyes and curly hair and beard. Water flowed out of its mouth into a half-circle basin with the flat edge pushed up flush against the wall. One of the most cherished symbols of Rome today is the *Bocca della Verita*, a disk-shaped flat mask that was originally thought to be a drain cover owing to its size. But it was in fact a very large fluvial outlet for a public plaza or park in ancient times.

Bowls of both circular and hemispherical fountains were built into the earth or paving at a low point to accentuate the height of the spout. The inner surfaces were sealed with a form of concrete called *opus signinum* that acted as a waterproof sealer.

Traditionally these surfaces were painted blue, much like contemporary swimming pools, to make the water appear more pure. Fish and other sea life were often painted on the inside of the fountain, so that the rippling water made the fish appear animated. This is particularly true in the large pools of the emperors. In these, the inner surfaces were lined with elaborate colorful mosaics, while the rest of the fountain was veneered in white travertine marble.

All these innovations yielded by the Roman love affair with water have contributed to the design and applications of our modern fountains. The Romans invented the pressurized water system and applied it on a massive scale. They created the tiered "Spanish" fountain and space-saving wall

ABOVE LEFT, This French
fountain features an
above-ground basin
that encloses a shallow
pool of water without
excavations.
ABOVE RIGHT, This
fountain illustrates the
subterranean basin,
which allows the water
to sit at or below grade.

fountains. They added classical sculpture to these water features and decorated them beautifully. And this foundation in the ancient world allowed
the great artisans of the Renaissance to create even bigger and more spectacular water works in the Italian mountains and the plains of France.

Modern Structural Concerns

It is important to begin by distinguishing between prefabricated portable
fountains and permanent, in-ground systems. This not only points out the
opportunities for creative design, it also brings up practical issues, such as
cost and maintenance.

Most fountains share the same components as the ancient fountains
we've described. They have a basin and a water source of some type, and
it is the form of these two components that defines the character and quality of the fountain. It is often the case that the basin itself is constructed
in place, and the water source is composed of a prefabricated decorative
component.

The Basin

Grade is a term given to the level of the earth at a given site, or the level
of paving surfaces, whether proposed or preexisting. This becomes the
starting point, or a vertical ground zero, for determining construction that
will occur above grade or subgrade (below the landscape).

A typical swimming pool is constructed subgrade—the earth around
the shell provides support for the weight and pressure of the water. Sub-

grade fountain basins are not very common, because they have some associated drainage issues. For example, the surrounding surfaces must not drain into the basin. Because the water is already below ground, you must pump or siphon out the water to drain the basin, which can require a good deal of extra plumbing.

The majority of fountains, both ancient and contemporary, are above grade. These require strong walls to enclose the body of water. They must be perfectly waterproof, or the moisture and minerals will seep through and stain the outside surfaces. The height of the walls may vary—from just a few inches for a true bowl-like effect, to much higher on monumental works. However, no matter how large the fountain, its walls are limited by the human scale and by the ability of people to view the water from any given point around the fountain.

In the residential fountain environment, the elevated basin can serve a more significant role than simply enclosing a body of water. The opportunity to configure that wall to double as a convenient seat is not only a more efficient use of space; it helps defer the cost of the fountain into other values in the finished landscape. These walls are ideally from about 18 inches (about 46 cm) tall to the optimal 2 feet (about 61 cm), and for comfort the cap should be two courses of brick wide, or about 18 inches.

It's common to find above-grade fountain bowls constructed as part of a system of raised planters and retaining walls. This is the ultimate integration of the fountain into a landscape and is very common in wall fountain or fluvial outlet styles. If there are preexisting walls, these will dictate the materials you should use in the fountain construction so that everything is well coordinated. If the preexisting masonry is lacking in style or material, it may be veneered along with the fountain so that the final product is perfectly coordinated.

These walls can be constructed in a variety of ways, depending on the local climate limitations. Certainly regions with severe winters will require specialized construction to ensure that the masonry remains intact through the rigors of freeze and thaw. These walls are usually constructed

HYDRAULICS SIMPLIFIED

Two important terms are vital to understanding the engineering of fountains and other water features. They dictate the required diameters of pipes and the size of the pump necessary to make the fountain appear a certain way.

Velocity

Velocity refers to the speed of water flowing past a given point. It is often described in cubic feet per second (CFS).

Head Pressure, or Feet of Head

Head pressure describes the force of water pressure relative to gravity, defined as pounds per square inch (PSI). The PSI determines how high a given amount of water can be pushed at a given pressure in a pipe of a given diameter. Head pressure is expressed in vertical feet. For example, at 60 PSI, water in a ½-inch- (12.5-mm-) diameter pipe can be pumped up 5 vertical feet (about 2 m) before it begins to lose pressure.

of a functional and structural core material; then a veneer material, such as tile or brick, is applied to make the wall more attractive and link it to the rest of the landscape.

Walls of fountains and their associated planters and footings are generally constructed of either concrete block or poured concrete, just like a pool or spa. They are usually covered with a veneer of brick, stone, or tile. Block is the most common because masons are quite familiar with this adaptable material. Poured concrete, however, is particularly valuable for curved walls that will be left exposed in more modern or minimalist applications in which block is unfeasible. It is also easily tinted when mixed to give a poured wall permanent coloring. Extensive wood forms must be constructed by skilled carpenters to create a high-quality poured wall with an attractive surface.

There are also prefabricated formal fountain basins that may be constructed virtually anywhere, often without a footing. These may be a single basin, or larger ones may be sold in components. Masons simply assemble the components into the finished product rather than requiring a high degree of craftsmanship to create such works from scratch.

The Fountainhead

The water source is the beating heart of the fountain. It is the artistic element that defines the character of the feature—unlike the basin, which is more functional. The volume of water that flows through the fountainhead, and the way it is sent out through the air, establishes the animated quality. This is the most variable element, reflective of many styles and eras—but it is the Renaissance contributions that dominate the market because their forms and decoration are timeless and perennially beautiful.

Fountainheads are produced in a variety of materials that vary drastically in price. They range from cast concrete on the low end to carved stone and bronze and other metals on the high end. In most residential applications, cast concrete is the material of choice owing both to wide adaptability and low cost. It is cast into an enormous assortment of forms and a multitude of decorative styles.

Until recently, a backyard fountain was less than feasible because it required the mechanical expenses of pumps and plumbing. In the last decade or so, the tiny submersible pumps and associated improvements in small-scale hydraulic equipment have made fountains available to practically everyone. This, in turn, caused the cast concrete industry to expand beyond its old market of lawn gnomes and religious images to offer some of the most beautiful designs of the Renaissance water works.

RESIDENTIAL FOUNTAINS ARE most often enjoyed up close, and you'll be able to scrutinize every nook and cranny of the creation. Take some time to consider less ordinary ideas. Use three-dimensional extruded color tile borders or bands, or even accented corner tiles. Explore architectural salvage for antique terra-cotta building ornaments to be combined with brick or stone. The options are limited only by your imagination—so while you are spending so much to create the perfect fountain, why not make it uniquely your own with the little things that count?

The standard approach is to construct the bowl or pool using the methods detailed thus far to serve a particular cast concrete fountainhead. It is important to choose the fountainhead first in order to design the appropriate bowl that matches in scale, design, and color. The appropriate ratio of bowl size to that of the prefabricated fountainhead is crucial to the overall proportions and balance of the final creation.

Concrete fountainheads always look best when they are well finished. There are techniques that make the concrete look like weathered white marble, or perhaps honey-colored limestone. The fountainhead can also be finished to mimic metals, such as copper verdigris. A likeness to expensive bronze can be created with the black of cast iron French designs. The single most important factor in the believ-ability of a faux-finished concrete fountainhead is the richness and depth of the coloring. Even a very simple concrete fountainhead can be made to look marvelous by merely applying a high-quality faux finish.

Carved stone is considerably more expensive than cast concrete, but it can exhibit a far greater level of decorative detail. Stone does not usually need special finishes because it is beautiful even in its fresh-cut condition, and ages beautifully over time.

Stone is also the choice for many contemporary fountainheads that are modern and abstract (different from the classical designs). This is some-times polished marble, which produces a shiny surface over which water can flow like glass. You may find the Japanese tea garden stone bowl inspi-rational in this category, using very simple form for its stark and dramatic effect.

Brass fountainheads are expensive, and because brass is subject to cor-rosion there are inherent problems when it is used in conjunction with water. Before you invest in a bronze or cast iron fountain, be sure you are working with a reputable professional who not only knows the materials, but has an ongoing relationship with the manufacturers.

Cast iron is an unusually brittle material that is easily cracked when mishandled—and such cracks are very difficult, if not impossible, to repair. In addition, seepage through irregularities in the casting can cause rust to set in. While these are the highest-quality fountainheads you can choose from in terms of design detail, they are also tricky to transport and install. Ultimately this is reflected in costs.

The most expensive type of fountain is made of bronze. Bronze is an alloy of copper and tin, the longest-lasting of the metals. The best bronzes

come from Italy or France, and although antique bronze fountains are almost impossible to find, the quality reproductions are nearly identical.

Within the last 10 years reproductions of old antique bronze fountains have crept into the upscale residential market. They are usually recast in Thailand using the lost-wax method. This method allows wax casts of old fountains to be made and then poured in new bronze. These casts are then finished to create an antique appearance using various acids. Reproductions look almost as good as the originals and are as long-lasting at less than half the price.

Bronze fountains add an incomparable look to the landscape. As they age, a blue-green patina develops on the surface of the metal to enhance and add depth to the decoration. With the exception of limited surface rust due to the effects of acid finishes, bronze fountains are not subject to structural rusting. They require no special care once installed and will remain beautiful and functional for centuries.

Cast iron fountains also add Old World charm to a landscape. These fountains are vulnerable to rusting and deteriorate if not adequately sealed

ABOVE LEFT, This series
of jets was inspired by
the long, narrow
fountains of the Middle
East and the Moorish
gardens of Spain.
ABOVE RIGHT, This long,
narrow pool with
pencil-thin jets evokes
the water features of
the Middle Eastern
influence.

and painted. A primer of anti-rusting agent must first be applied under the finish coat of epoxy paint. Only after the primer and epoxy are in place can oil-based paints be applied. This final outer coat can be rubbed off to create a faux antique appearance. You can expect to repaint and reseal a cast iron fountain every five years.

Both cast iron and bronze fountains tend to be extraordinarily heavy. A crane or forklift may be required to lift these fountains onto their prospective bases. Some cast iron fountains can be purchased with precast iron water basins, but they are not necessary. In fact, the excessive weight of iron bases is problematic on a residential level. It is preferable to construct a permanent masonry basin for these fountains, then install the fountainhead.

The Art of Water Sculpture

Water sculpture is a term used to describe the art of manipulating water while it is suspended in the air. Clearly, to achieve the proper effect requires that the fountain be fed at a high rate of pressure. These techniques have been developed over centuries and remained in the fountain maker's toolbox because they are tried and true. An endless assortment of water sculpture patterns exists, many perfected in 19th-century France, but not all are feasible in today's market. They may not prove cost effective, or are simply too complex to fabricate in a residential setting.

The most important problem concerning water sculpture fountains is wind. Persistent prevailing winds can distort the shape of the fountain spray pattern and perpetually mar its beauty. This also causes drift of the water drops well outside the basin area, which creates a new set of problems. Downwind paving areas can become wet and slippery. It can also cause permanent staining of the pavement over time, particularly in communities with water quality problems, or where it is damp enough for algae and molds to take hold in perpetually moist masonry.

Before deciding on a water sculpture for your site, take the wind direction and speed and seasons of highest velocity into consideration. You can mitigate some of these effects by choosing fountainheads that use a heavy stream spray rather than those that disperse the water into drops, which are more easily carried away. If there is still a problem, you had best rethink the water feature and design it in a more wind-resistant form that is less dependent on water sculpture for its beauty.

In general, your fountain designer will be able to select from certain forms that are available in prefabricated fountainhead units. These bronze heads eliminate the need to engineer the effect anew with each fountain. Although you can endlessly explore alternatives and custom effects, it is unlikely that fabrication of the fountainhead will prove cost effective, or a significant improvement upon the tried-and-true commercially manufactured heads.

Pressurized fountainheads are collectively known as *jets*, which are sold under common names that roughly describe the shape or form of the overall effect. These terms are recognized throughout the industry and will help you better understand their different applications. Each may be one, two, or a dozen or more jets set into a single fountainhead at precision points to achieve the desired effect. Once again, it is far better to choose a prefabricated fountain jet than to try to start from scratch.

- *Cascade jets.* Create a highly aerated, conical water pattern with frothy texture that is reflective and creates the most dramatic effect when lighted
- *Smooth-bore jets.* Designed to produce a high, straight stream with minimal breakup and limited drift in windy conditions
- *Spray rings.* Circular tube with equally spaced holes or jets along its entire length that create a vertical fall, an inside fall, or a cross pattern
- *Fleur-de-lis jets.* Produce a graceful multiple-tiered pattern of distinct streams to create a flowerlike effect
- *Fan jets.* Align a vertical row of jets to produce a fanlike pattern of distinct water streams
- *Umbrella or mushroom jets.* Produce a clear, unbroken sheet of water falling in a circular pattern for a dome effect
- *Spherical peacock jets.* Create lacy, shimmering spheres of water that maintain their precise and pleasing contours while staying in constant motion

Fountain jets vary in size from large commercial models to small residential ones. Because the residential fountain market is exploding, more and more residential-scale products are available. The larger and more dramatic fountain jets are constructed of cast bronze and may be suitable for high-end residential or commercial water features. These require large basins to accommodate the spray patterns and water drift under windy conditions. Smaller residential fountain jets are composed of UV light–resistant molded plastic and are much better adapted to fountains in small spaces.

A Few Words About Spray

The wilder and more animated the fountain, the greater its potential to spray water outside its designated area. Sometimes it's the result of windy conditions, or of turning up the flow rate to create more sound. No matter what the source, this is a problem you should know about, because spray can raise some safety and aesthetic issues.

Fountains located close to windows and sliding glass doors can cause water spotting on the glass, particularly in windy areas. A design with a well-defined stream, rather than a mist or fan spray, is wind resistant. It will, however, cause splash in the basin below. Splash tends to plague designs with very shallow basins lacking strong edges to intercept the droplets.

Spotting on glass, whether due to wind drift of droplets or oversplash of larger drops, is a big problem in neighborhoods with hard water. It leaves behind a visible mineral residue when each drop dries on the window, just as it does on kitchen glasses. You should be sure that the fountain is positioned properly to prevent an everyday problem, but be prepared for occasional high winds to cause spots.

A fountain in high-traffic areas produces overspray onto adjacent paved surfaces. This will result in different problems, depending on exposure and duration. Algae may bloom on moist paving, which can cause discoloration—though some gardeners love that green, mossy patina that gives it an old, weathered look. Be cautious if you want the paving to remain crisp and bright as the day it was laid. For many, the solution is to place pots or planting around the immediate edges of the fountain so that overspray will go onto the plants, not the paving.

Beware of algae-coated paving, because it can become slippery. Once established in the masonry, algae can multiply quickly during the rainy season when your fountain may overflow. If the fountain is in a high-traffic location and algae grows around it, you may suddenly encounter a hazardous surface. This is why understanding traffic patterns around your fountain is so crucial.

Water Quality and Algae

The Old World water works were often created with a flow-through water system. Water would flow through the fountain and continue onward to a new destination. No water was recirculated, which kept the fountains free of disfiguring algae. Algae do not find fast-moving water an ideal environment, and prefer to grow in slow-moving or still water.

The single biggest threat to your fountain water quality is one of the most primitive plant groups on earth. There are over seven thousand species of green algae, and vast numbers of brown and red algae as well. These tenacious organisms survive in some of the most inhospitable places on earth, such as the boiling water of hot spring geysers and the permafrost of the Arctic. The differences among the individual species are so minute that we group them all together when considering their presence in water features.

Like other plants, most algae are green because they contain chlorophyll and depend on sunlight for food production. They also need oxygen to carry on the photosynthetic processes. Some types of algae are single celled, while others consist of just a few cells in a string or cluster. They

Formal pools with
plants and fish create a
unique character that
reflects sky and garden
in a constantly changing
mirror image.

have the ability to reproduce rapidly if conditions are right. Ideally they thrive when three needs are met: sunlight, warm water temperatures, and high nitrate concentrations in the water.

Even single cells of algae, invisible to the naked eye, will become highly visible when their numbers reach concentrated levels. The point at which they are so numerous as to change the color of the water is called *algae bloom*. The most familiar example of algae bloom is a poorly maintained swimming pool that turns green as the water quality deteriorates.

When the population of algae grows to even larger numbers, the organisms come together in "rafts" that may float on the surface or accumulate around the water's edge. These huge colonies are often perceived to be a single slimy plant, but are actually a whole community of them. They prefer to exist closer to the surface, exposed to unobstructed sunlight and high oxygen levels.

Algae will also flourish in porous masonry surfaces. After a swimming pool has suffered a serious algae infestation, vestiges of that algae remain dormant in the plaster. As soon as chemical levels fall below a certain potency they come to life again. This is why a pool is more difficult to maintain after its first incidence of algae bloom. Algae flourishes in fountain masonry as well, and will bloom overnight as water warms up.

Algae is considered attractive when a natural or antique look is desired in a water feature. In more formalized fountains it can provide freshly carved stone with that wonderful patina of age. (We'll discuss the role of algae in staining natural waterfalls later in the book.) Over time the various types of algae will impregnate the masonry and mortar to produce a patchwork of subtly varying hues that is naturally beautiful.

For those who want a crisper or modern style, though, algae can be a serious problem. It has a tendency to build up around spouts, where there's an abundance of oxygen and sunlight. In fact, gradual accumulation of algae at the openings of fountain spouts can eventually narrow that orifice and reduce the flow rates. Lower flows mean the fountain will not function at its optimal level.

Fountains can be divided into two categories that are defined by algae. A fountain that is simply an aesthetic feature can be easily kept algae-free by simply adding a regular dose of chlorine. Because people don't swim in fountains, the chemical balance need not be as exact as that of a swimming pool. The only requirement is that the chlorine levels not fall below that required to control algae bloom. The treatment may be as simple as adding a tablet or a liquid product once a month or whenever the water first appears to change color. This may seem obvious, but remember that you *cannot grow water plants or keep fish* in such treated water.

The second type of fountain is one that does support plants and fish. These are not necessarily a traditional water garden, but may support just one papyrus or lily. They may also contain some goldfish or mosquito fish to control insect larvae. Algae will tend to bloom in warm weather when the waste from fish and the organic matter from plants raises nitrogen con-

A small pool with aquatic plants can make a perfect centerpiece for a larger formal garden. It may be used as a still pool or may be piped with a single small jet for a very different character.

tent to critical levels. These fountains can be cleaned out periodically or the water replaced as often as needed to ensure clarity and discourage algae.

A traditional water garden that supports a diversity of plants and fish year-round must maintain a delicate balance. These tend to be larger and less easily cleaned, or the quantity of water they hold makes it challenging to replace the water. In this case you may have to install some type of filtration system, which increases both installation cost and maintenance of the filter. The filter is usually connected to the circulating waterfall or fountain pump, so it does not usually require its own pump.

For chronic algae problems, consider resorting to an organic aquatic algicide product. These are effective in treating algae, but be sure the one you choose is also nontoxic to fish. Because algae are plants, there may be collateral damage to other plants living in the treated water. Highly sensitive plants, such as water lettuce or lilies, may prove more vulnerable to effects of algicides than other reedlike plants. The golden rule is to verify that the product should be harmless to fish *and plants* before introducing it into the water. Otherwise, you can store the plants in another water-filled container while you treat the water, and return them to the fountain only after the product has degraded to nonthreatening proportions.

There is no right or wrong concerning your individual water quality strategy. Obviously, whether you have water plants or fish will be the deciding factor. Decide how much time you are willing to invest in the maintenance of those water plants. People who travel may find the unexpected algae bloom too much to cope with upon their return.

It's OK to start out small to see for yourself how much maintenance is generated from season to season in your local climate zone. Try some reeds, then the more perishable water lilies and floating plants. If it proves too much, simply throw out the plants and change to a more sterile, chlorinated water.

This illustrates why it is important that the fountain is designed to be equally attractive with or without plants. Like the Romans, who added painted fish and mosaics to their fountains, make sure yours is beautiful in its own right when nestled amidst surroundings of terrestrial plantings on dry ground around it. The more these plants drape over the edges—or, in the case of vines, weave into the fountain itself—the less you need water plants to green it up.

Position and Impact

There is no question that your fountain will become a pivotal feature in your landscape, courtyard, or atrium. Once constructed, it cannot be moved, so it is crucial to consider every possibility to ensure it is accurately positioned to maximize the impact on surrounding spaces.

The *line of sight* from living spaces both inside and outdoors varies. The perspective changes if you are on the ground floor or if you will view the fountain from above. All of these factors influence the position and the layout of the fountain itself. A tier fountain is gorgeous when seen from the ground plain, but from above it becomes one-dimensional, with its best features hidden underneath. A water sculpture fountain may provide tremendous interest from above when jets produce interesting water patterns.

This pool and its fountain sculpture have been precisely positioned to be framed by the arched opening, in a direct line of sight from this sheltered outdoor living space.

Similarly, a fountain designed for viewing while you are seated on the patio or indoors must be low to the ground so you need not look up too far to clear the sides of the basin. Always think in three dimensions in order to be responsive to all these design concerns.

Because a fountain is so expensive, its visual connection to interior spaces makes it a benefit both indoors and out. Sometimes a foot or two (30 to 60 cm) either way will make a big difference in how you see it through a particular door or window. It's always interesting to find a water feature that greets the visitor when first entering the house, or that may be discovered unexpectedly as one turns a corner. In some cases the fountain is more subtly tucked into the landscape to enhance the space without overwhelming it. Fountains should never appear as though they were placed by accident—they must seem to naturally belong.

The visual impact of any fountain lies in part with the water and with its decorative elements. Again, in the old Roman designs, symbols and motifs reflected cultural meaning. Fluvial outlets featured masks of river gods. Fountain spouts resembled mythical animals and fertility symbols such as the pinecone. Later the baroque influence led to excessive detailing featuring cherubs, nymphs, and goddesses plus various water-related animal motifs.

Not every space or landscape is suited to these classical styles. Modern minimalism and fountains that rely on more contemporary sculptures are often more in keeping with architecture or garden, or even personal taste. These do not offer such spectacular decoration, but there is great drama in simple lines that do not compete with the natural beauty of the water but enhance its fluid movement.

Positioning, like fountain type, can be assessed according to intended use of the adjacent spaces. Each basic arrangement has its assets and liabilities, but above all they relate to functionality in terms of both the surrounding usable space, and their point of maximized visibility.

Central Rear

This arrangement places the fountain in the center of the view, but pushed back to the rear of the space for a more efficient layout without sacrificing usage. It will draw the eye outward from the immediate vicinity to the depths of the garden, through both sight and sound. This increases the sense of space, better connecting it to doorways to the interior that may be open. It is important that the fountain be sized in proportion to the depth of this field to prevent it from appearing dominant rather than a more desirable, subtle focal point. This is an excellent design relationship for smaller lots seeking to create the illusion of greater space and maximize the usable area outdoors.

Center

This is the design of the traditional Spanish courtyard that was surrounded by buildings on all sides. It is usually a tiered style and the walls of the basin serve as additional seating. The tiers of water add humidity to the air to modify the microclimate by creating a cooler, protected outdoor space in hot climates. These fountains are often highly decorated to make them even more interesting, because at close range these courtyard spaces have no outward or alternative views. In addition,

This formal fountain is perfectly centered between the columns of the pergola behind. The two art nouveau sculptures that flank the columns reinforce this visual and highly symmetrical relationship.

the views from the windows and doors looking outward to the space will be dominated by the mass and presence of the fountain. This position is not an efficient use of space and is best used in larger gardens or courtyards and patios.

Central Foreground

This position can be a valuable tool for dividing very large spaces into smaller ones that are more controlled. If the indoor rooms or patios need a more immediate focal point to separate the intimacy around the house from an expansive yard, then the central foreground position is ideal. Though it does not obscure the view beyond, its presence demands that the viewer first consider it before going onward.

This may also be a valuable tool for water features on view lots with a need for a more intimate space. In very warm climates, such as that of Southern California, these smaller fountains make a view a lot more inviting during the heat of the day. You may also need something closer up to capture your interest on the patio and provide a feature around which to arrange an attractive planting plan. At night these water features provide a valuable subject for night lighting, particularly when the view is so rural that it turns black after dark without city lights.

Side Walls

This position is most often applied when you do not want the fountain directly in the line of sight. This is the case if there is already a focal point in the garden or an attractive view beyond. When you want the users' attention to be drawn elsewhere, you can compel it with a side-positioned fountain. It offers the opportunity to create a second axis in the patio or garden to foil a too-linear scenario. There is an exciting dynamic that is created in gardens with more than one axis, and the use of wall fountains makes this achievable in smaller spaces.

Bird's-Eye View

It is not often that we have the opportunity to see our fountains from above, or what architects call "plan view." In the past many great garden makers of Europe did have the opportunity when gazing out the windows on the upper floors of Blenheim Palace and Versailles. The value of rigid geometry became paramount in these applications, which did not necessarily offer much to those witnessing them on the ground plain. Most designs created from this perspective are more decorative and rely on symmetry and motifs to keep us interested. Again, it is not common that we have the chance to design for a bird's-eye view, but it is intriguing to discover how European royalty maximized these effects.

THE FORMAL FOUNTAIN AFTER DARK
Design by Michael Glassman

THE GRACE AND elegance of formal fountains are beautiful by day, but they can become magical by night. Michael Glassman's designs feature very formal fountains created for the ultimate in custom residential effects. What makes this water feature so special is its versatility and the changeable environment for nighttime viewing and outdoor entertaining on a grand scale.

ALL ARCHITECTURE IS GREAT ARCHITECTURE AFTER SUNSET; PERHAPS ARCHITECTURE IS REALLY A NOCTURNAL ART, LIKE THE ART OF FIREWORKS.

—G. K. CHESTERTON, *TREMENDOUS TRIFLES*, 1909

The home features a large central pool with a formal fountain. At the center of the pool stands an enormous open-pedestal urn, its stem piped for water in the old Roman technique. As the design evolved, the enormous pedestal urn required a sufficiently large pool beneath, and after its dimensions were thoroughly reviewed it was decided that perhaps it should graduate to something more than a fountain. This also related to the question of water quality and size, making it cost effective to upgrade to a swimming pool.

This formal fountain may be controlled to produce a variety of effects by varying the rate of the flow. This is the peak flow rate of the central water column, which creates a solid but luxurious effect.

Opposite, Jets mounted into the four corners of the swimming pool shoot into the open urn in the center. The jets help to cool the air under the arbors and add a more active and festive effect that is dramatic as seen through the living area windows.

Though small in swimming pool terms, the result was a useful fountain that could be enjoyed on a whole new level during the heat of the summer.

The central urn, the heart of the water feature, functions in a number of ways that influence both its visibility and the degree of sound it produces. The owner need only adjust the flow by a remote control to achieve any one or a combination of possibilities. Such a changeable fountain makes it better suited to each season or to a particular social milieu, from a languid summer afternoon card party to a black-tie dinner dance on the terrace. High flow rates provide the swimmer with an added dimension as well.

The water is forced up through the urn, and at the slowest rate it simply overflows into the pool beneath. The next setting creates a small frothing spout in the center, and the other sequential phases raise that into pressurized water columns of various heights. This pool is also fitted with hidden corner jets that are equally adjustable. They may be set to shoot into the middle of the urn or any other distance within the pool. Ultimately the owner may mix and match water column heights with jet distances for a different effect at any time.

The living spaces around this water feature are generously sized and complemented by a full outdoor kitchen complete with granite countertops. The fountain is lighted to make the water works visible at night, and illumination of the adjacent spaces is subtle so as not to create competition.

This entire fountain is consummately fitted with the latest in outdoor lighting to maximize its visibility and dynamic action after dark. Lights inside the urn itself shine up through the water column from underneath. Swimming pool lights set into the pool walls underwater illuminate its contents in a soft, even glow. Directional lights mounted on the adjacent arbor allow these high-intensity beams to perfectly light corner jets, and to better call attention to the shape and decoration of the outside of the urn.

This beautiful fountain evokes the best and most applicable Old World water design concepts. It employs the pedestal urn of Roman fountains, a sculptural water column favored by the French, and jets used so efficiently in Middle Eastern designs. Coupled with well-crafted night lighting, this is the consummate formal feature that can be enjoyed indoors, outdoors, and even inside the water.

Elegance and Old World Charm

The permanent formal fountain is not for everyone or every garden. The expense can be considerable when you add design fees, construction, and prefabricated fountainheads, particularly when constructed of bronze. But when you wish to create something lasting that will enhance the overall character and value of an upscale homesite, there is nothing else that is so reliably successful.

Formality is a statement that is deeply appealing in terms of its elegance and Old World charm. The designs popular centuries and even millennia ago remain as compellingly beautiful and timely today. This illustrates the longevity of formality, which can be relied upon to transcend the coming and going of design fads, just as classical concertos have survived the emergence of so many other musical styles.

YOU CAN'T HOPE TO PERSUADE US THAT NATURE BUILT THE HOUSE, WHY INSULT
OUR UNDERSTANDING BY PRETENDING THAT NATURE MADE THE GARDEN? . . . IT
MAY BE ARGUED FURTHER THAT REAL BEAUTY IS NEITHER IN GARDEN NOR
LANDSCAPE, BUT IN THE RELATION OF BOTH TO THE INDIVIDUAL, THAT WHAT WE ARE
SEEKING IS NOT ONLY A SCENIC SETTING FOR POOL AND FOUNTAIN AND PARTERRE,
BUT A BACKGROUND FOR LIFE.
—SIR GEORGE SITWELL, *ON THE MAKING OF GARDENS, 1909*

THE STYLIZED FOUNTAIN

HUMAN BEINGS and their cultures are beautifully reflected in the way their gardens and fountains are designed. The fountain tells the history of the people, it reflects their religious beliefs, and it suggests what was important in life. Because the spectacle of water has been a part of nearly every culture on earth, there exists a wonderful diversity of expression. Each tells a story and each is capable of re-creating the same ambience as once existed in its place of origin.

We who dwell in homes and gardens share a personal vision of the ultimate environment. It is a purely subjective thing, a preference that may be born of our childhood, of an inherent romanticism, or perhaps simply of the affinity for a particular architectural

A Gallery of Stylized Fountains

There is an endless variety of stylized fountains both new and old that exists throughout the world. Each one is a unique expression of design that provides us with inspiration for ever more innovative compositions.

The Grotto

This is a very old European idea that first emerged in ancient times. A grotto is merely the opening to a cave, and very often it was a damp place where shade and water encouraged certain types of plants. Sometimes the water came from above the cave, or it may have issued out of the mouth of it. In mythology grottoes were often viewed as sanctuaries of gods and goddesses, and even entrances to the underworld. This is the reason why such a feature was called a *nymphaeum*, for it was considered the realm of the water nymphs.

A traditional Italian fern-cloaked grotto is constructed of stone and concrete. Over many years the creeping roots of ferns permeate the walls, where there is perpetual moisture and shade.

This imbued grottoes with more than just natural or physical interest, adding a romantic and spiritual dimension.

Artificially created grottoes are found most often today in Italian gardens built into hillsides or slopes. They are usually made of stone and concrete to create a damp dripping place as respite from the often hot, dry climate. During the Renaissance, secluded water-filled grottoes were often integrated into great pleasure gardens, sequestered in an area where one could retreat from the heat and noise for a contemplative environment. Often the grottoes include classical sculptures of Greco-Roman gods, which identify these places as spiritually important.

What characterizes the grotto as a garden feature is the planting. In naturally wet, wild grottoes, a variety of ferns and mosses colonize into the nooks and crannies of a cliff face. Their roots actually provide anchorage on near-vertical surfaces so that over time the stone itself is completely shrouded in foliage, ferns, mosses, and cliff-dwelling plants. Creation of an artificial grotto has long used a very porous mixture of stone and concrete. When first built, they are not particularly attractive, but after the plants become established the true beauty emerges.

FAR LEFT, Although
beautiful, fountainheads
such as this
are works of art and
extremely expensive.
AT LEFT, In Mexico City
this hillside features a
fountainhead carved in
the image of the Aztec
god as a unifying
symbol of cultural
history. TOP RIGHT, This
patio fountain features
old clay pots in many
shapes and sizes as the
artistic element. Water
flows up through the
pots to overflow into the
pool below. The pots are
nestled in clumps of
cattails and surrounded
by the sharp contrast of
a closely sheared
boxwood hedge.

Art and Artifact

Stylized fountain design is often at its best when the water feature expresses itself in cultural art. This expression may be quite clear, as in the case of the Tepeyac Hill fountains in Mexico City. Located on the rocky hillside below a Catholic shrine, the water spouts that feed the water works are channeled through a series of spouts inspired by pre-Columbian art. The spouts are made of carved stone depicting the stone mask of the Aztec god Quetzalcoatl, also known as the plumed serpent. The mask expresses the spirituality of pre-Columbian Mexico within the context of a contemporary Catholic holy site. Such a blending of imagery endows the spouts with more than mere visual interest, suggesting a deeper spiritual truth of a people.

Artifact is also an important component in stylized fountains. Ceramic pots, which are made and used around the world, provide graceful architectural forms as well as water-holding vessels. Integration of such containers into stylized fountain settings provides an assortment of choices in size, shape, and finish glazes, each suggesting a slightly different character.

Bamboo

The use of bamboo in stylized water features is unique to the Asian-inspired garden. It does not fall into the large landscapes with their waterfalls and pools, but functions in a more intimate setting. The bamboo spout adds unique color and simplicity to the basin, usually of carved stone or creatively shaped cast concrete. These are not highly visible, and evolved out of the need for freshwater to continually circulate through the basin. A secondary application for bamboo was designed to frighten deer out of the garden. The bamboo spout is fitted into a pivoting arm, and when it becomes full enough it falls with the weight of the water to strike an empty bamboo pipe. This sudden noise and movement are capable of deterring wildlife that would otherwise browse on the plants.

Islamic Wall Fountain

This type of stylized fountain is rooted in the gardens of the Middle East, where a lack of water made its usage highly valuable. There was so little to spare for plants and beloved flowers that the people developed very bright ceramic tiles that could substitute. The geometric patterns evolved because their religion forbade the depiction of graven images, and therefore they developed intensely bright and complex designs. Ultimately this style of water feature, functional in providing the household with water and beautiful in its color, became the genesis for many of the Mediterranean- and Spanish-style water features we see today. Incidentally, the beautiful patterns woven into their famous wool carpets sought to depict gardens in their designs as well. While living in such a climate made growing plants for ornament too great a luxury, they covered the floors

ABOVE LEFT, The traditional fountains of the Middle East rely on the color of ceramic tile patterns instead of thirsty flowers. Very little water flows, but it echoes against the walls of the courtyard. ABOVE RIGHT, The postmodern movement has influenced fountain designs by integrating vibrant colors and creative sculptural elements. BELOW RIGHT, A detail of a relief tile band shows elaborate contemporary ceramics that may be used in creation of new fountains modeled after much older ideas.

with gardens of wool just as they created walls of flowers in patterns of ceramic tile.

Modern and Postmodern

The contemporary style is rooted in two 20th-century design movements: the modernist era and the more recent postmodern trend. Modern design is highly minimalist, with clear, clean lines that lack ornament, except perhaps bold colors and lines. The postmodern era is more eclectic and draws its inspiration from architectural history, including such ancient elements as Egyptian columns and Greco-Roman pediments. These design trends are more frequently seen in civic water features than in residential ones, but they do indeed exist and are highly appealing as an adjunct to contemporary architecture.

Wall-Mounted Fountain Concerns

Wall-mounted fountains require a very different setup strategy because they require no foundation but hang on a vertical surface. This presents a

MIRACULOUS MOSQUITO FISH

MOSQUITOES EXIST IN most regions, and shallow water features can provide an ideal breeding ground in certain seasons. These insects tend to flourish in still, shallow water, and their very rapid life cycle can cause a serious problem in a few short weeks. Small, guppylike mosquito fish (*Gambusa affinis*) are effective weapons against waterborne mosquito larvae. They are efficient feeders that will keep fountains and pools larvae-free for an entire season even when there is no filter system in place. If you change the water periodically, simply net the fish, store in a bucket, and replace when you're through. Some communities offer free mosquito fish through their agricultural departments or mosquito abatement boards to anyone with a body of water likely to house larvae. Many garden centers or water garden specialty stores offer inexpensive mosquito fish that are an excellent natural solution to this perennial water garden problem.

host of challenges that are more difficult to resolve with larger, heavier fountains.

Installation methods depend on whether you will mount the fountain on a masonry wall, a wood core stucco wall, or a wood fence. The weight of the fountain, which can be considerable when full of water, demands that the wall or fence be structurally intact and well anchored.

To hang a wall fountain on a concrete or masonry wall, drill out an anchor hole with a diamond tip masonry drill bit. Then countersink a galvanized masonry shield onto the wall, and screw a galvanized hook or bolt into the orifice on the shield. Seal all the edges with plumber's silicone to prevent water running down the wall to collect behind the shield.

To hang a wall fountain on a wood core stucco wall or on drywall, use a molly bolt or toggle bolt. These will expand and hold the hook tightly to the wall without pulling away. It's essential that you thoroughly seal this hole with plenty of plumber's silicone so that water cannot enter the inside of the wall. If it does, over time the wood will rot and so weaken that the whole molly bolt will pull out with the slightest pressure. It's always best to hire someone knowledgeable to hang a wall fountain, particularly if the wall is part of your house or garage. Damage can cause structural weakness, discoloration, or problems with electrical systems and plumbing that run through these walls.

It's easy to sink a mounting bolt into a wood fence, but larger problems arise if the fence is not strong enough to support the weight of the fountain. Although a fence may appear to be structurally sound, the posts often rot at or just below the soil line. Rotted posts can break or disintegrate under the strain of even the lightest fountains. Another hazard is inadequate framing, or weakness due to long-term exposure to the elements. This makes wood shrink, crack, and warp, and loosens the connections, resulting in a wobbly, unstable fence.

The best solution for making a fence better able to withstand the weight of a fountain is to simply reinforce it. You need not rebuild the entire fence—only the panel or post where you mount the fountain. One alternative is to sink a new post behind the fence where it is out of view. Drill through the fence to anchor for the mounting bolt into the new post so that it alone supports the fountain. There are many different ways to achieve this same end that will vary with the design of the existing fence and the demands of the new fountain.

An important thing to remember about wall fountains is that the cord will protrude from the bottom of the back panel. When it is mounted on a surface with preexisting openings, such as lattice, you can simply thread the cord out the back. When it is mounted on a wood fence, drill a hole for the cord to thread it through to the back side.

Walls made of plaster or stucco are more challenging. The rule of thumb is that you never drill into them if it can be avoided, because this can provide an avenue for damaging moisture to penetrate the wall. If there is no alternative but to drill a hole, be sure there is plenty of weatherproof glue to create a tight, long-lasting seal between the cord and the surrounding hole.

If the cord cannot be routed elsewhere, it will have to run down the face of the wall, where it is highly visible, all the way to the wall socket. In this scenario your only choice is to disguise both cord and socket as well as you can.

Plants are the best and most logical solution for disguising dangling cords and exposed sockets. Plants belong around the fountain anyway as a design tool for enhancing its natural beauty through a living garden composition. With some careful planning, you can make then serve a dual purpose. The key is to use plants beneath the fountain that grow tall enough to mask the cord but won't grow so high that they envelop the fountain itself. If the plug is nearby, you must be sure the planting is wide enough to block it too.

If no in-ground planting area is available, use a gathering of attractive well-planted pots. It's not uncommon to use groups of pots in an eye-catching composition of differing heights for a great deal of interest and versatility. Pots also allow you the flexibility of rearranging them with the season or with your whim. Use many different sizes, with big beautifully crafted pots for drama surrounded by smaller ones you can arrange just so to cover socket and cord.

Stylish Versus Trendy

Your water feature or fountain will invariably fall into categories described in this chapter, or other categories we have not explored here. Yet styles as the inspiration for fountain design have clearly transcended centuries, if not millennia, proving the solid basis of the aesthetic criteria. It is essential that you understand this, because the amount of money you will spend to construct a stylized fountain should not be wasted on a design that will appear out of date and inappropriate in just a few years.

Using a large preexisting pine tree, this beautiful chain and bell fountain evokes the peaceful harmony of Zen. The water is simply pumped up to the top of the bell chain, then flows down and is collected in the glazed ceramic pot at the base. This is an excellent design for gardens with little floor space to spare but plenty of vertical space to work with.

It is always best to risk too conservative a design than to find yourself with an outlandish creation that will quickly become an eyesore. Beware of new and unusual products that reflect a very contemporary character, because they will be the first to show their age. In the landscape, where water is concerned, it is the visibility of the water that we seek, which should never be eclipsed by its delivery system.

If you do not feel confident in your own ability to identify timeless design, do not feel inadequate—in most cases, a homeowner is not expected to have such a keen eye. The secret is to seek out a competent local designer, landscape architect, or architect who will guide you in the direction that complements your landscape, your house, and your lifestyle. Be sure to view firsthand examples of his or her work to ensure you find the style appealing. The professional's ability to create water features within the constraints of local soils and weather is crucial to long-term success. Keep in mind that many professionals are expert in certain types of styles, while others exhibit a more eclectic proficiency.

Once again, a stylized fountain will be expensive in both design and construction. However, this will be offset by the increase in property values that is incumbent with any well-made amenity. In the meantime, it will offer you many years of satisfaction as you enjoy a water-filled environment that enhances outdoor living and provides a beautiful focal point for both house and garden.

NEW ORLEANS COURTYARD
Design by Michael Glassman

THIS CITY OF the Old South was founded by the Spanish, then became a French colony, and finally fell into American hands in the early 19th century with the Louisiana Purchase. Its architecture today evokes both of its European legacies, with thick-walled Spanish-style houses organized around central outdoor courtyards. Such enclosure prevented an outward view, thus forcing the eye to remain within a tightly bounded space. There the need for interest was paramount, and gave birth to ironwork creations rooted in the elaborate French formal style and classical detailing.

TO FILL THAT SPACE WITH OBJECTS OF BEAUTY, TO DELIGHT THE EYE AFTER IT HAS BEEN STRUCK, TO FIX THE ATTENTION WHERE IT HAS BEEN CAUGHT, TO PROLONG ASTONISHMENT INTO ADMIRATION, ARE PURPOSES NOT UNWORTHY OF THE GREATEST DESIGNS.
—HUMPHREY REPTON, *THE ART OF LANDSCAPE GARDENING*, 1795

The courtyards of New Orleans were once vital spaces for living in an impossibly hot, humid climate. They nearly always featured a fountain, either as a central feature or pushed up against a wall where space was limited. The fountain provided water for drinking and washing at first, then after city water became common they reverted to strictly ornamental status.

New Orleans often reflected its French heritage with cast iron fountainheads in Old World style bearing the details and intricate design characteristic of the Empire period. Planting is decidedly tropical, as that city experiences no frost. Thus, the combination of exotic plants, European styling, and strong architectural presence defines the character of these urban places.

This small brick corner house was situated in an older American neighborhood where shade trees had reached mammoth proportions. It was bordered by an alley to the rear, by a street on one side, and by a neighbor on the opposite side. On that alley corner adjacent to the neighbor stood a small stucco single-car garage that was not particularly attractive but did provide a convenient screen. The backyard depth was exceptionally narrow, producing a shoebox-like space that ran the length of the rear of the house. A single immense redwood tree dominated the north end of the space and provided comfortable shade on hot summer days.

The palette of materials was assembled based on that of the house so that all would be coordinated into a seamless whole. The red brick of the house with white trim at the doors and windows offered rich colors. However, the combination of the brick and the shadows of the redwood tree's evergreen foliage tended to darken the space by absorbing light. The chief goal of

This reproduction cast iron fountain was inspired by antique designs found in both Paris and New Orleans. Although brand new, it evokes that time-worn patina from day one. The small pool is easy to maintain without a filter and supports aquatic plants and fish.

designer Michael Glassman was to integrate brighter value materials that would magnify the light without sacrificing shade.

Michael chose to introduce a third construction material, soft pink Arizona flagstone. This effect can be matched in colder climates by pink granite or other locally produced pale colored flagstone that does not absorb heat. Whenever possible, other components of the site would be whitewash, not only to better tie into the architecture, but so that the coloring would reflect sunlight without radiating heat.

The flagstone is accented by the red brick. In paving it serves as an edge ribbon and is featured on all steps. The caps on the seatwalls are also brick, a more user-friendly bull-nose unit.

This landscape focused on two spaces: one for seating and the other dominated by a central fountain. Each is defined by low walls that enclose raised planting areas to reduce maintenance while offering more outdoor seating. Elevated planting areas also allow improved soil to be added to counter worn-out natural soil deeper down. This improved planting medium allowed for a more successful perennial flower garden than if it had been constructed on grade.

Elevated planters could not be used at the redwood tree because soil must never be piled up against the base of a tree trunk. Raising grade at the base of the trunk causes direct contact of earth to the bark, which will initiate rotting and death of the vital cambium layer underneath. If the cambium rots all the way around the trunk, the tree will die. Therefore, the walls in this garden were designed with close attention to finish grades in order to provide plenty of raised high-profile planting without risk to the health of the redwood.

Rather than just one, there are a number of focal points in this garden. The fountain is the primary feature, designed after the small New Orleans style, which utilizes a permanent in-ground basin with matching raised walls. The fountainhead itself is cast iron in the traditional French style, incorporating two separate tiers. Cast iron allows a thinner, less massive fountain in smaller spaces because of its natural structural integrity. The fine detailing is much more appropriate in this setting, where its intricacies can be appreciated close up.

Over time this cast iron fountain will develop a marked patina that combines mineral deposits with algae stains and inevitable rust spots. Nothing comes close to this great textured surface, and it is particularly beautiful when combined with bright green plants. It is interesting to note that the plants in this water feature are grown in pots that are separate from the surrounding pool water. This allows the owners to treat the water with algicide, if they wish, without sacrificing the plants.

Beyond the fountain is a portable spa, unobtrusively tucked into a corner between the gate and redwood tree. Its high-quality wood housing matches nicely with redwood tree bark and the other materials of the landscape with their warm, soft hues. This is a beautiful example of how a portable spa is designed into the landscape, not treated as an afterthought. The fountain becomes a beautiful focal point for those relaxing in the spa or dining at the table on the opposite side.

The view of the other end of the garden is dominated by the garage. Michael's goal was to transform it from a bare wall to a real focal point itself

Small fountains are well suited to pond comets, the very inexpensive goldfish that will survive outdoors. They are smaller than koi and much less costly if you lose a few. The fountain helps to keep the water circulating and well aerated for the fish. The rushes and umbrella grass used here are some of the toughest water plants and are ideal for beginners.

by providing an illusion. First the mass of the wall was broken up into panels, which were then veneered with a white lattice. The center panel, larger than the others, became a canvas where an artist has painted a fantasy view from the terrace of a coastal Mediterranean villa. Its sense of depth creates a trompe l'oeil. The mural is visible from every part of the landscape, and it creates the mood that inspired a planted landscape of both exotic plants and traditional European species.

In the large planting area in the foreground of the mural grow a selection of very dramatic flowering perennials that are sun-loving and festive. Flower colors were chosen to blend believably with the hues of the mural in order to enhance the trompe l'oeil effect. Tall blood-red penstemon hybrids are spectacular in foliage and flower color, drawing hummingbirds in droves. Peach and yellow daylilies fill the beds, along with white Shasta daisies and other easy-to-grow perennials.

Featured in the raised planting areas are a pair of beautiful corkscrew Italian cypress trees that are preformed by the grower into perfect sculptures. These are combined with citrus trees and other evergreens in sun-drenched areas uninfluenced by the massive coast redwood tree.

Underneath its acidic canopy grow a wholly different group of plants that thrive in the shade and soil condition of the forest floor. Ferns and impatiens offer foliage and flowers beneath a specimen of bushy South American angel's trumpet (*Brugmansia*), which produces gorgeous foot-long trumpet flowers periodically throughout the year.

This little city landscape offers beauty at every turn. It is intimately private owing to white lattice fencing that extends higher than the standard 6 feet (about 2 m). As planting matures, much of this fence will disappear behind a cloak of green foliage and colorful flowers. The whole space is filled with the sound of water from the charming fountain, and the faux view of the mural suggests there is more beyond than simply the neighbor's yard.

While inspired by New Orleans, featuring Mediterranean scenery, this landscape indeed creates a holistic stylized environment that carries its occupants instantly away from the surrounding lot and block subdivision. It is a tiny excursion into a fantasy environment that naturally evokes a more peaceful place and time through plants and water.

The mural painted on the bare wall of the garage fools the eye into perceiving a view rather than a utility building. Perennial flowers in the foreground help to make it appear even more realistic. Murals are a valuable tool for solving problems in small spaces surrounded by oppressive buildings.

Rewards of Great Design

Great water feature design rests on a foundation built of skill and self-knowledge. Many believe we do not really come to know our personal preferences until after age 40, and until then our sense of beauty and taste is in a perpetual state of flux. Only after we have perhaps traveled a bit, or experienced a diversity of environments both natural and built, do we come to recognize the manifestation of our inner self.

You may spend a good deal of money on your water-filled garden. Therefore, when all the construction is completed, you must know the results will be intensely satisfying. The emphasis, then, is far greater on design of the fountain itself than on construction. You must allow sufficient time to explore all the possible alternatives before breaking ground. Do not rush the process. Do not leave any aspect of it to chance, and don't hesitate to change the plans. In reality it will prove much easier and far less expensive to erase and redraw a fountain on paper than it is to demolish and start again when it fails to move you in the landscape.

THE POOL IS A PLACE TO GATHER AROUND, MUCH AS A FIREPLACE IS IN A ROOM.
—THOMAS D. CHURCH, *GARDENS ARE FOR PEOPLE*, 1955

SWIMMING *in the* GARDEN

IT CAN BE SAID that the legacy of the communal Roman bath is the contemporary swimming pool. Though it is not designed for hygiene, the modern pool offers a very similar social environment. Until the advent of the affordable swimming pool, water in gardens was rare because of the maintenance requirements of a feature that was merely aesthetic.

The swimming pool, once sequestered on estates or featured at swanky resort hotels, has since World War II become a common sight in suburban communities. This is particularly so in warm climates, such as Southern California and Florida, in which

This is the old-style American swimming pool with its typical kidney shape, precast coping edge, white plaster, and requisite aqua waterline tile.

pools may be used year-round. Yet swimming pools are not limited to warm regions but are found in every state, from New England to the desert Southwest.

It is clear that water touches us in a primal way, and the mere sight of it in the heat of a summer's day has a subliminal effect on the human psyche. Where a natural water feature may appear beautiful, it does not beckon us to become one with it, to enter that green depth for pure physical enjoyment. But a swimming pool, with its crystal clear water, holds no hidden surprises, and its transparency relieves us of all hesitation to abandon ourselves to its cooling, refreshing effects.

As the swimming pool has evolved over the past few decades, it has changed through technological advances to appear more integrated with its surroundings. Early pools contained a very depressed water level so that the *freeboard*, or the distance between the water surface and that of the surrounding paved area, could be as much as 2 feet (about 61 cm). The pools were rectangular and laid out to preestablished proportions and depths, forcing virtually every one to appear identical to the next.

The rectangular form was rooted in history, inspired by the reflection pools at Versailles and by the Moorish water features of Granada, Spain. On a more practical side, the shoebox shape was favored by the emerging Olympic sport of competitive swimming that required square ends for an efficient high-speed turn. Actor and Olympic medalist Johnny Weissmuller as Tarzan would soon bring freestyle swimming into virtually every American home.

By the 1950s the swimming pool had lost much of its freeboard so that the water level was just 6 to 8 inches (about 15 to 20 cm) below the surface of surrounding paving. This made an important visual difference.

This new level allowed one to view a deck and the water beyond as more of a seamless whole, with only a subtle color difference between the paving and blue water.

This era, with its strong tendency toward modernist minimalism, introduced long sweeping lines to the swimming pool just as it did to architecture and landscape design. Pools graduated from basic rectangular forms to the famous "kidney" shape, which proved more flexible and compatible with less formal landscaping. However, the proportions of the kidney pool remained static, while only size and orientation changed from site to site.

This was the postwar era, when the American population exploded and landscape architects began to design homesites very differently. The essence of this design revolution changed the driving force of the layout to feature the site as a whole living space, not one to contain house or pool in isolation. The focus was on places where growing families could live, dine, and play outdoors. The vision of the nuclear family in the American suburbs, particularly those in the Sun Belt, evolved into an expansive recreational backyard in which the pool was the most vital component of all.

Swimming pool emphasis, and the problems of forcing rectangular- and kidney-shaped pools into problematic yards, demanded some changes. While pool contractors previously learned to create just two basic shapes, the public screamed for variety. Even if they lived in the typical housing tract, many wanted a pool unique to their home and landscape. Ultimately the change would be wrought by landscape architects such as Thomas Church, who would design a completely unique pool shape for each project rather than relying on preset forms. It was this early work that precipitated the transition of swimming pools from mere amenity to an artistic element of the landscape.

Suddenly swimming pools became responsive to the site, rather than requiring the site to adapt to pool configurations. The pool was designed in tandem with living spaces and planting in a holistic environment. The pool was still the focus of the landscape, but was no longer forced on the landscape.

Powerful Pool Design

The past few decades have seen a period of seminal change in pool design, with special design features becoming affordable in the middle-income residential setting. New decking materials, tiles, elevated edges, and plaster colors contribute a host of fresh aesthetic options. Some of them vastly increase the cost of the pool, while others may reduce it. In many cases you can build an attractive, innovative swimming pool for the same price as an average one by seeking out the cutting-edge options. These will go a long way in making water work harder within the landscape.

The key to success is to learn where and how you can make your pool project something special. In this chapter you will discover how to design so the pool fits your personal needs and those of your family. Don't settle for standard practices when you can manipulate spatial relationships and components to your advantage. Most of all, you will be able to spend that considerable sum of money knowing it will yield a beautiful amenity that enhances the environmental quality and enjoyment of your home.

Functionality

A swimming pool is not just an aesthetic amenity, but a useful body of water. It may serve a social use that keeps the kids home at play in their own safe backyard. Pools are growing as a means of regular nonimpact exercise, such as water aerobics or lap swimming, plus healthy therapies. The pool is also a feature that encourages social interaction on a more pas-sive adult level. Each of these uses establishes functional criteria that directs its ultimate design.

There are three basic features of the pool that influence its function. First is the shape; second, the depth; and third, the arrangement of space adjacent to the pool. As we explore the various uses, you will discover how these three factors dictate what the functional pool will look like.

Solving the Exercise Problem

Pools as a source of exercise are one of the fastest-growing applications because many Americans are growing older and can no longer enjoy high-impact sports. The need for cardiovascular conditioning and muscle ton-

ABOVE LEFT, This pool is designed to be viewed from the adjacent living spaces out of sight at the left. The disappearing edge bond beam is invisible and makes the water blend naturally into the planting beyond without any interruption from paving or constructed elements on the far side. ABOVE RIGHT, While this pool is under construction, you can see its "bones" before it is plastered.

POOL TERMINOLOGY

Bond Beam

This is the thick wall of concrete, steel, and plumbing that produces the permanent shell of your pool underground. A raised bond beam is a custom pool option that raises all or part of that shell above the level of the surrounding grade or paving.

Decking

This term applies to any surfacing that surrounds your swimming pool, whether it is wood or not. It may vary in area from just a few feet wide to expansive patios that serve as outdoor living spaces. This surface is almost always some kind of concrete, stone, or masonry unit, such as brick. All pool decking must bear a slip-resistant surface texture to make it safe.

Coping

This surfacing is the immediate edge of the pool that covers the top of the bond beam and cantilevers a few inches over the water. Old pools from the 1950s and earlier used precast coping units that were uniform among all pools. New pools may use expensive stone coping for special effects. Most pools today reduce costs by eliminating coping units altogether. The pool deck is created in a single pour of concrete that not only covers the bond beam but is cantilevered over the water edge as well.

Waterline Tile

This is the band of tile set into the plaster wall of the pool just below the coping. Water levels in the pool are kept at about the middle of the tile band. Fluctuating water will deposit scum and mineral buildup at the waterline, and glazed ceramic surfaces are much easier to keep clean than plaster. This tile was originally a standard monochromatic sky blue, but in 1970s vintage pools we find "Spanish" patterns and other alternative colors. Today the trend is back to the elegance of monochrome tile, with a good deal of latitude in colors.

Swim-Out

This is a bench or ledge, or sometimes steps, integrated into the inner wall of the pool. These are useful features that eliminate the ugly chrome metal ladders so common in the deep end of old pools. Swim-outs do not interfere with the pool's geometry, allowing swimmers to get in and out of the deep end. They also offer swimmers a convenient place to rest and socialize beyond the limited shallow-end steps.

The raised bond beam extends the pool wall to create a higher-elevation patio. The waterline tile—blue, 2-inch square, with white grout—extends along the waterline at the left, then rises with the bond beam to create an easy-to-clean face. The coping is cantilevered and veneered with gray paving stone and the pool plaster is white, which gives the water its characteristic turquoise color.

ing is crucial to health at any age—but for the elderly or people with disabilities, swimming proves to be the most sustainable of all activities. Many seniors choose a shallow pool in order to facilitate such exercises rather than a traditional pool with shallow and deep ends.

Lap swimming dictates its own criteria, with the overall length being the most vital concern. The longer the pool, the less often the swimmer must turn. A standard competition-length pool is 25 yards (75 feet, about 23 m) in length. This is a very long pool by residential standards, and few lots are large enough to allow it. In most cases the deciding force is the length of the backyard, and the concern is how to maximize the pool within the constraints.

Lap pools bring us back to the long, narrow troughs of the Spanish garden influenced by the Middle Eastern style. With their rigid geometry, they are well adapted to semiformal gardens, and the pool can be made more aesthetically interesting through small spouts and brightly colored tiles. More and more Americans are opting for lap pools, particularly those in homes on narrow but deep lots.

The second factor that is often overlooked is the turning area. If you are an experienced swimmer, you may execute flip turns, which require a minimum depth of 2 feet 9 inches (about 84 cm), but 3 feet (about 91 cm) to 3 feet 6 inches (about 1 m 6 cm) is considered the standard. It is best to turn on a flat wall at both ends that is easy to push off from. You cannot do flip turns where there are steps, so be sure the design places them away from turning areas at both ends of the pool.

Another less common but easily constructed feature helps lap swimmers gauge their point of turn. Competition pools feature tiles, usually black, set into the wall of the pool to keep the swimmer on course. The wall tile actually helps the swimmer's eye gauge the changing, shrinking distance to the wall. It is a small and inexpensive feature to add to a new pool construction, but for the user it promises a far more effective workout.

Finally, it is important to realize that a lap pool need not be rectangular. You can build a free-form pool for lap swimming so long as there are two opposing points that constitute the "lane." To better identify the lane, the tile set into each end of the lane (as described in the previous paragraph) is even more important in keeping the swimmer on track. This is also a much more aesthetically pleasing alternative to functional but unattractive lane line tiles across the bottom of the pool, which can spoil a naturalistic design.

Lap pools require great length, but limited width, and may be pushed up against property lines to maximize the usability of the adjacent outdoor living spaces.

A second emerging form of swimming pool exercise is water aerobics. This is a valuable therapy for those who are too weak to exercise on dry land or are not well suited to lap swimming. Water aerobics requires a shallow bottom because the user is most often standing up. This means that there should be adequate area in the shallow end to accommodate the user (or users). For many, the best solution is a slightly deeper area at the center of the pool that transitions up to shallow on both ends.

Avoiding a Dangerous Dive

Diving is an activity enjoyed by children and adults alike. Competition diving is a growing sport in many high schools and colleges that offer swimming programs. Diving at home, particularly challenging competition diving, may require a special pool design to be safe. The depth of the pool must be greater than average for a competition board, and this factor should be fully understood by both the pool designer and the contractor who will build it. To achieve such a depth the dimensions of the pool must be altered to conform to building standards. It is essential to the safety and success of the new pool that this be clearly understood from the outset of the project.

Recreational diving is safe with a standard-depth pool according to the National Spa and Pool Institute, although recent evidence suggests that while such depths may be ideal for children, teens and adults may be at risk. The problem is not in the depth of the deep end, but at the transitional ramp where the bottom slopes up to meet the shallow end. Strong adults push off the board and hit the water closer to the shallow end than children do. The solution is not to add depth, but to reduce the size of the shallow end so that the ramp begins to angle upward much farther from the board.

Diving boards are always at the center of the argument over function versus aesthetics. Boards are not particularly attractive, and they take up a lot of room. Shorter miniboards have become real problem-solvers in small spaces, but they do not give the user much spring for challenging dives. They do, however, allow a board where no other board would be possible.

An alternative to boards for a more aesthetic diving experience is the incorporation of diving rocks into the edge of naturalistic pools, or of raised bond beams that give swimmers a higher point to jump from. But neither provides much cantilever, and both lack spring. There is an increased chance of a user hitting his or her head on the pool edge if the dive or jump is not well executed because of the lack of significant cantilever.

It is important to make these diving points and boards safe. This requires attention to the entire route of the user from the jumping-off point to the water. Slip-resistant paving and steps are crucial. Beware of river-rounded diving boulders, which can become slippery when wet. It is always better to use rougher stone or to employ a stone mason to rough up that surface for more secure footing.

Keep the point at which you exit the water in mind when designing a diving pool. It should be close to the board or diving place so that the users must travel just a short distance. Children at play tend to run from the exit to the board, and the longer their trip, the greater the chance of a slip. Remember also to ensure plenty of vertical room above the diving board. This eliminates the chance of bumping one's head on a house eave or tree branch during a particularly hard bounce.

Better Fun and Games

Family pools remain the consummate place to play on hot summer days for adults and kids alike. The use may range from formal water games to entertaining toddlers. Pool design is variable but should suit both present needs and those of the future as the children grow up.

The most important feature that influences how and where we play in pools is depth. It is also vitally important to safety. Today's smaller lots have given birth to play-oriented family pools that simply lack a deep end. This discourages diving and the fears associated with accidents.

The new pool bottom profile is slightly deeper in the middle with two opposing shallow ends. This is appealing to adults who are not good swimmers and would like to be able to touch the bottom at all points in the pool. It also maximizes the amount of area suited to very small children or new swimmers.

Such a design is perfect for water volleyball, water polo, and other organized sports. It allows the net to be strung across the middle of the pool, leaving the shallow ends for both teams to stand and play without treading water.

Another Kind of Living Space

Swimming pools present another kind of entertainment value for adults when the homesite is small. This is important wherever there are very high summer temperatures, particularly at night. The pool can be designed as an actual outdoor living space where users may sit comfortably in the water for conversation, cocktails, and even casual dining. In fact, the pools at Mexico's most exclusive resort hotels have bar stools integrated into the pool itself so that guests can enjoy drinks or dining while still in the water.

Sitting in the pool requires surfaces that are made for that purpose. They should be at a depth that is comfortable, and most are about that of a swim-out. Locate these around the edge of the pool to directly interact with the patios, cook centers, and other major gathering points in the landscape. Swim-out seating will increase the comfort of your guests and maximize the use of the pool during get-togethers and parties. For socialization, size is also important. Unlike the in/out function of a swim-out, you may want to provide enough space for two or three people to sit together without feeling crowded.

Another variation on this swim-out concept is called a *beach*. Rather than traditional steps into the shallow end, the beach is a hyperextension of the second step fanning out at a very gentle angle to mimic the ramp of a natural sandy beach. This serves as a social gathering place, but it was originally developed to better help small children learn to swim. The beach provides plenty of room to play and become accustomed to deepening water without having to step off a sharply edged step.

Solutions for the Style-Conscious

Swimming pool design is a powerful tool for creating just the kind of landscape style you're looking for. Few people live in houses with custom architecture, but if you are lucky enough to dwell in a Spanish-style stucco home, a Victorian, or a prim colonial, your pool design should reflect some of the characteristics of these themes.

If you live in a house with mundane architecture, or one of the millions of older generic tract homes in America, you have two choices. The first is to extend what you have done with interior design into the landscape to create a pool that is appropriate in form and material. The fact that most pools lie directly in the view of the back windows of a house suggests that sometimes the interior is the most appropriate influence. It is often the family room or kitchen with this view, and therefore your interior design character, not the architectural facade, is the best guide for pool design.

The other option is to create a separate exterior experience that is not so responsive to the house or its interior. This approach allows you a clean slate to create the pool landscape of your dreams. This is a growing trend because a fantasy backyard getaway is valuable therapy for a busy lifestyle.

Among the more popular examples are a South Pacific lagoon, a woodland spring glade, or a sun-drenched Tuscan villa garden. The scenario need not fall into a particular category but may evolve out of your personal preferences of materials and color. The surrounding landscape will be vital to achieving a holistic effect so that the pool, garden, and living spaces all support one another to create a beautiful, restful environment.

COMPONENTS OF STYLE

THE BEST-RECOGNIZED styles are created using key materials and plants. Though not essential, they are a good starting point when designing your own special environment.

Asia

Pool: Irregular shape, milled stone paving, fine gravel walks, embossed glazed Ming-green tile, gentle waterfall or bamboo spout

Accents: Granite/concrete tea garden basin, pagoda lights, bright antique urns

Plants: Bamboo, dwarf conifers pruned to bonsai, azaleas, flowering cherry tree

Mediterranean

Pool: Square or rectangular long narrow shape, terra-cotta pavers, colorful Spanish tiles, opposing stream spouts, mask spout

Accents: Antique stoneware urns, classical accent art, lots of terra-cotta pots and sculpture

Plants: Lavender, sweet bay tree, oleander, bougainvillea, rosemary, boxwood

South Pacific

Pool: Rounded shape, rough flagstone, earthtone tiles, rock waterfalls

Accents: Southeast Asian art pieces, woven bamboo panels, or rods in pots

Plants: Palms, flowering vines, hibiscus, large-leafed exotics

English Cottage

Pool: Rectangular or circular geometric, smooth granite pavers, red brick accents, reflective water surface

Accents: Potted citrus and topiary

Plants: Riot of perennials, old-fashioned flowering shrubs, flowering vines

TOP, A fantasy pool inspired by tropical plants may not be for everyone but illustrates a surrealistic approach tailored to the night swimmer. MIDDLE, A South Pacific lagoon is the inspiration for this pool built around a preexisting volcanic rock outcropping. BOTTOM, The English style features roses and perennial flowers in a riot of color.

POSTMODERN MAKEOVER
Design by Michael Glassman

THE POSTMODERN MOVEMENT found its roots in the powerful applications of color in cubist and abstract art. Architects such as Luis Barragán of Mexico began grand experiments in color, both on the building skin and in the landscape itself. The power of walls bearing bold hues blended with a natural landscape of blessed neutral green produced for Barragán the dynamic that is so beautifully created in this poolside landscape.

WHY DO TWO COLORS, PUT ONE NEXT TO THE OTHER, SING? CAN ONE REALLY EXPLAIN THIS? NO.
—PABLO PICASSO, *PICASSO ON ART*, 1972

OPPOSITE, The simple geometry of clean rectangular lines is timeless, but even the most beautiful pool requires remodeling with time. Simply replacing the old, tired pool deck with clean poured and textured concrete gave it a sharp, modern upgrade. The large open space found order through a new focal point, the custom-designed fountain that lent a greater sense of presence to the old preexisting swimming pool.

The house began like so many other postwar tract homes on large lots. An expansive lot, a family swimming pool, and a lawn constituted its chief outdoor amenities. The homeowners were connoisseurs of modern art, and their remodel of the building itself transformed tract architecture into a bold statement featuring the curves and color characteristic of the postmodern movement that rose in the 1980s. The remodel was designed by Sacramento architect Steven Goldstein, who developed the color palette that is reflected in the landscape.

The finished home featured gently curved stucco walls bearing contemporary windows trimmed in snow white, which virtually leap out of the solid-colored fields. The exterior colors used by Michael Glassman became an extension of the interior spaces, which also shared the very bold color schemes of the exterior facade.

The challenge of this landscape was to re-create the worn-out traditional swimming pool and yard into a sun-filled space that integrated indoors and out. The result was a dramatic composition that utilizes simple planes and forms with bold, high-contrast colors to produce an outstanding design.

The chief problem with the landscape was that the whole backyard lacked a focal point. The pool proved far too large and simple to become an interest point by itself. There had to be something more profound and in keeping with the artistic themes indoors to provide something to look out on from living and dining spaces. The decision was to create a fountain that was visually tied to the pool but wholly separate in order to retain the pool's simple yet dramatic form.

The pool's lazy L shape seemed to point to the end of the backyard with the most available space. There Michael designed a large, sprawling fountain structure that proved simple in its conception but a bit more difficult in its

In order to cut costs, the special Indian slate paving was limited to the high-traffic, high-visibility outdoor living area. Recessed lighting on the step face helps to identify the subtle grade change where the slate meets the textured concrete pool deck. This slate is a multicolored stone that provides a broad range of hues tying into many of the featured architectural colors.

construction. A series of low interconnected walls of varying height were designed to create both a foundation and a symmetrical framework for the central sheet waterfall. The face of the waterfall was veneered in blue-violet glazed ceramic tile that also provided the working surface for the outdoor cooking center.

Three different heights of wall were used, each bearing a different color. These frame the central sculpture, a stylized modernist mother and child. It was created out of salvage steel by local sculptor Jennifer Johnson. The dark rusty finish stands in dramatic contrast against the bright-colored walls.

The main backing for the water feature was a single coral-red panel slightly curved for reverse dish effect. This was flanked by two separate side panels in a reverse curve of golden almond color. Both curves reflect the sweeping arch of the remodeled rear facade of the house. To better transition to the ground plain, the third pair of walls, constructed in a mint green stucco, provide additional poolside seating.

This same mint-green color was linked with a series of raised planters on the opposite end of the pool and integrated into the building itself. These planter walls enclose the main outdoor living space and provide additional wall seating. Inset lighting helps to call attention to the muted green walls after dark.

The central living space that is accessed by the kitchen door is a high-intensity outdoor dining environment that integrates interior colors and materials perfectly. The overhead structure constructed of square steel reflects custom ironwork used indoors. It is painted white to draw from window trim and match the balcony railing of the second story. Support posts are poured concrete

Opposite, This remodel of a postwar tract house into a contemporary work of art rests on bold forms and a palette of vivid colors that coordinate with the interior design scheme. The color palette was reflected in the new green wall planters, the violet tile of the outdoor cooking center, and the mellow gold accent.

Opposite, The design and location of the new focal point fountain is wholly responsive to the end of the preexisting swimming pool, but is not connected with it. The back walls provide variety in height, depth, and color to better coordinate with the house. At left, Simple drama defines this composition, which relies on the power of contrasting color and bold geometric forms. The water flows over a weir with precision to create a clean water curtain as crisp as the walls that flank it. The lip is capped with Indian slate and the face of the wall is veneered with easy-to-clean glazed ceramic tile. The dark finish of the modern sculpture stands out dramatically against the coral background.

painted black to match the post of the house's front entry portico to better integrate the front yard architectural features into the rear portion of the site.

Indoor floors are surfaced with a steel gray slate, which is matched outdoors by a more colorful Indian slate. To reduce costs, this expensive stone surface was limited to the dining areas, then steps down onto secondary concrete paving at the pool deck.

The pool deck is poured concrete tinted a soft apricot color, also drawn from the interior design color palette. Simple expansion joints and a salt finish provide very little interruption of this field of color that is in striking contrast with the turquoise of the pool water.

Planting schemes for this landscape are simple, resting in the broad range of green in a variety of plant textures. The fountain was provided with a coast redwood evergreen privacy screen. All flowering plants on site were chosen to match the overall scheme of coral, yellow, violet, white, and purple.

Despite the postmodern splendor of this fabulous landscape, it is actually a very simple design created with even more ordinary materials. What sets it off is the power of color, and as Picasso said, it is the dynamic of placing one high-contrast color against another to create the subtle visual vibration that excites the human subconscious. There is little here but concrete block, stucco, paint, and steel, yet by combining them together Michael has created a monumental work of environmental art.

Spatial Relationships and Pool Layout

After you have explored how your pool will function and its general style or character, it is essential that you understand some basic ideas governing pool layout and construction. You need not learn everything here; the pool contractor or designer will be able to help you with most of these decisions. But you don't want them to make all your decisions for you, because it's important to retain some control over your own project. After all, when the contractor is long gone, you're the one who must live with the pool.

There are some important features in every pool, and these are also the most changeable parts of the pool. When chosen well, they can lend character to your pool. You have a great deal of latitude with materials and finishes that can be very effective, even on a budget. But if you don't know your choices, you'll end up with the option that makes the contractor his greatest profit margin.

Bond Beam Magic

The bond beam is not just the essential shell of the pool—it is a very useful tool for solving some of the most vexing site problems. The basic shell of the pool does not change, but when the bond beam is raised above this original profile, it can act as a retaining wall to allow the surface behind it to be elevated above that of the rest of the deck.

A raised bond beam is frequently used to integrate the pool wall into a series of planters. This is often when the pool must be pushed up against the backyard property line in order to maximize the amount of patio living space between the back of the house and the nearest pool edge. Often the bond beam sits right on the lot's rear setback line, and the remainder of the area behind is devoted to planting. This is typically the solution for cut-and-fill view lots with only a limited backyard area pushed up against a steep-cut slope.

The raised bond beam also produces a *face*, which is the highly visible area between the waterline tile and the top of the wall. A variety of treatments for this face use creative materials for better visual quality. Most pool walls are constructed with concrete block above the waterline, depending on the application. The block is frequently veneered with brick or bricklike units, but wherever there is a lot of splash there will be a perennial risk of white mineral buildup that is difficult to remove from such porous materials.

The face can be veneered with ceramic tile that is easy to keep clean. Tile, manufactured in a rainbow of colors, offers an incredible range of design options. More creative applications use a unique combination of colors to produce bands of contrast—or something more avant-garde, such as checkerboard. Tile murals sold as an integral series are also popular, particularly in Mediterranean- or Spanish-inspired themes. This face of a raised bond beam can also be the perfect opportunity to create a special water feature.

Deck

Besides the surface of the water, the deck is the most visible part of the pool area. The deck must be slip-resistant to be safe, so slick glazed tile or smooth marble surfaces are not suitable here. The basic material is poured concrete, which can be finished in a variety of ways. It can be colored, imprinted, and textured to mimic more expensive materials or to better match preexisting materials both indoors and out.

Other deck options include various types of natural flagstone, milled flagstone, textured tile, and brick or other types of precast pavers. This specialty deck adds expense because you are essentially paving twice, with the attractive veneer laid over a poured concrete base slab. Not only do you use twice the material, but the veneer will carry with it hefty shipping charges if not purchased locally. In addition, most of these require a very experienced mason to set them properly. Costs are increased by irregularly shaped natural flagstone, which can be problematic owing to variations in thickness.

Concrete remains the most common pool deck because it is remarkably versatile and requires only a single-layer application. Among the most popular applications at poolside is exposed aggregate, which is concrete that uses pea gravel in the mix. It's poured, and then the surface is immediately washed to remove the thin layer of cement. This reveals an even texture of gravel that is cooler to walk on and more slip- and stain-resistant than standard concrete finishes. You can specify different colors of gravel in the mix to achieve a gray, beige, or orange tone.

Another approach to decking is to color the concrete and then imprint the top with a pattern that looks like something more expensive. These

New techniques with poured concrete pool decking allow a clean edge and a surface that is colored, textured, and geometrically scored to add interest.

Stone slate coping with carefully coordinated waterline tile creates a perfectly matched edge condition featuring a rich range of hues.

techniques have come a long way in recent years, and now an experienced contractor can create a dead ringer for terra-cotta tile or milled stone using nothing but this straightforward technique. It is more expensive than a basic slab because of the time and work necessary to imprint a believable pattern, but it's still quite affordable compared to applying a second surface of veneer.

Coping

These days, we rarely use precast coping units on swimming pools, and many pools are built using a cantilevered slab. Though efficient and tidy, it does little to accent the shape of the pool; but many like the clean, modern lines. The alternative is more expensive accent coping that acts like a frame around a beautiful painting. What is attractive all by itself becomes magnificent in the right frame.

The most commonly used unit coping is brick with one end in a rounded or bull-nose shape. Bull-nose units were designed as a safer coping than square brick with its sharp corners. Bull-nose is not only safer, but more attractive. Most manufacturers offer bull-nose units with each of their decorative brick colors.

Coping for naturalistic pools can also be constructed out of the more expensive veneer stones. A natural pool deserves an irregular cantilevered flagstone edge to complete the picture. This is perhaps the most expensive option of all because of the skill required to set the material properly.

Waterline Tile

This feature is probably the most rewarding choice you'll make, but it can also be the most difficult. In the beginning, pools all shared the same sky blue tile, which was thought to best match the light blue color of the water. In those days no one would ever dream of considering even a mildly greenish tile, as it would imply there was an algae problem. People building swimming pools were trying to overcome visions of green farm ponds, and clarity was crucial.

In the 1970s the waterline tile market was dominated by Spanish-style tiles in keeping with the colorful, psychedelic fashions of the time. Although they were installed in backyard pools all across America, Spanish tile does not belong in most pool settings except those inspired by Mediterranean or Latin American style.

To make matters worse, increasingly elaborate patterns were originally printed in a single large tile. These became fragmented mosaics of smaller tiles set on a webbed fabric backing for easy installation. Although they were successful at first, individual pieces inevitably popped off and could not be replaced when the tile was discontinued. A tiny piece about 1 inch (about 25 mm) in size could be the undoing of an entire pool, or it was simply replaced with a similar-sized piece from a different pattern.

Today we have come back to the wisdom of the simple blue tile, but it is far more varied because we aren't so paranoid about the vague suggestion of algae. The tiles we choose from today are the old blues and blue-greens, but the manufacturers have made them more vivid, with luminescent color. Some feature subtle mottling that works far better with naturalistic looking dark-bottom pools or in conjunction with rock waterfalls.

Ultimately the tile you choose should correspond well with the color of your pool plaster and with other components in the landscape. Lighter colors correspond with white plaster, while darker hues are suited to dark plaster. You may choose large square tiles or thinner vertical tiles to add a bit more interest at the waterline.

Above all, the tile must be frostproof, which means it is dense and does not absorb water. This is crucial for all climates that experience frost, because tiles that absorb water suffer when that water freezes and expands. It is much better to choose your waterline tiles from those samples offered through your pool contractor, because he will only carry sufficiently frostproof ceramics.

WHY NOT WOOD?

IT IS RARE to find wood as pool decking because the chlorinated water will damage the surface and its coating of stain or preservative. Where wood deck is desirable, it should be separated from the pool by a band of concrete or masonry decking so that there is minimal damage to the wood.

Plaster

After the shell or bond beam of the pool is completed, the last step is to plaster the pool. Until the 1970s, all pools shared the familiar white plaster and turquoise water color. Then the energy crisis raised concerns over the cost of pool heating bills, and it was found that pools with darker bottoms were more quickly heated by the sun. Designers began to experiment with dark plaster in natural pools with a lot of rockwork, which was far more successful because the contrast between boulders and the artificially bright pool bottom just didn't work. The disadvantage of dark plaster was that it was too efficient in hot climates, causing the water to overheat.

Plaster also bears on how the pool looks after dark. Lighter plaster makes a pool far brighter at night when the pool lights are on. It glows like a turquoise gem to blind the eye to the spaces around it. Darker plaster makes the pool's presence far more subtle, and tends to keep the other appointments of the garden within visual perception.

Today we may choose from light or dark plasters, and a large number of shades in-between. Manipulating plaster color is a valuable tool for adding interest, contrast, and mood to a swimming pool. Darker plaster yields a more reflective pool surface that is like a formal water feature of England or France. It is ideal for use with pools featuring natural rocks and boulders, particularly when applied in an irregular patchwork of varying hue for a mottled appearance. Mottling does not appeal to everyone, however, so be sure to see some examples of these pools before committing your project.

There is no right or wrong when it comes to plaster color, but a wise choice takes into consideration the other materials at the waterline and the deck, the overall character of the pool, and its appeal in both daylight and night. Next to the decking itself, it is the most visible choice you can make to achieve the greatest visual potential of the entire setting.

Steps

Every pool must have steps for easy access. Though they are necessary to make the pool functional, they are also an important design element. The design of the pool can be further enhanced by the way the steps are laid out, because they are quite visible from most points around the deck.

There are three basic options for manipulating step design, and these mirror techniques used by landscape architects to lay out steps elsewhere in the dry landscape. The one aspect of the steps that cannot be changed is the riser height, which is usually consistent throughout the series.

First, you can change the layout of the steps to be rounded or square, depending on the character of the pool. Second, you can change the depth of the step tread so that the user descends into the water more slowly through a gradual transition.

Steps should reflect the character of the pool itself. A graceful free-form pool will look best with steps that are similarly curved. Hard geometric forms are complemented by equally rigid steps.

The third technique is to use glazed ceramic tiles inset into the plaster of the steps to add color. This is a good idea in terms of safety, particularly for those who are older or have poor vision. The contrasting tile punches up the edge of the step to make it far more visible, just as paint and tape are used to make public curbs and steps more apparent. Most of the time the waterline tile color is repeated at the steps—but where that tile has too little contrast to show up at depth, something bolder is called for.

Resort hotels have created some remarkable patterns on pool bottoms, both at steps and elsewhere, with mosaics. Small 1-inch (about 25-mm) gold tiles give the steps and bottom a glittery effect that is enhanced by night lighting, and these are often combined with similar-sized tiles in cobalt or royal blue for better contrast. A residential pool can also use some of these more festive or whimsical tile choices to line the steps and create a visually interesting entry experience. Adding them to creatively shaped steps produces a unique feature that gives even an average rectangular pool a custom look.

Lighting

The standard pool package typically includes minimal lighting within the pool itself. The number of fixtures and their position will vary, which makes this a good tool for creating a special mood or enhancing the over-all look.

The light fixtures are located in a niche in the structure of the pool that is properly grounded and bonded to prevent leakage. These lights may vary in size from 8 inches (about 20 cm) to 12 inches (about 30 cm) in diameter. The wattage, or the strength of the light produced, can range as

well, from 150 to 500 watts. Smaller lights tend to be used in smaller pools and spas, while larger ones are vital to illuminating very large or exceptionally long pools.

Pool lights are typically 110-volt incandescent fixtures that are GFI protected for safety. In recent years halogen fixtures have entered the residential market, but they are more expensive. Still, they require less electricity to operate, so they may save money in the long run.

Fiber optics have entered the swimming pool market in a big way. This type of lighting is created by shooting light through a multistrand cable. It is possible to make the light change color from green to red, for example, with revolving lens fittings or with special colored gels to create a more theatrical setting. The most common application is to run fiber-optic cable under the coping, hidden and tucked up at the top of the waterline tile. This sends light downward onto the waterline tile to illuminate its color after dark and to outline the general shape of the pool and emphasize its geometry. When specialty tile is used, this combination can be stunning. Although fiber optic lighting is a wonderful innovation, it is not often used owing to high installation costs.

Spouts and Jets

Water features for swimming pools and spas can use some less spectacular techniques that are just as dramatic. Once again, they are not new ideas, and their roots stretch far back in history. These features can be integrated into a pool in a more subtle way than a waterfall can, and are less expensive because they do not require such monumental plumbing and piping.

The terms *spouts* and *jets* relate to different kinds of effects. A *spout* is literally just an opening from which water flows, and it is usually in a downward position at relatively low pressure. A *jet* faces upward and shoots water at high pressure, like many of the famous fountains in city parks.

One of the most common scenarios for spouts occurs in pools with a raised bond beam along one side. These are most often built in small spaces where the pool is pushed to the back of the yard to sit right on the setback line. The raised bond beam provides a perfect support for spouts at virtually any point along its length. Each spout is piped to produce water that flows by gravity into the pool below. In some cases the spouts are made out of terra-cotta pipe and the water flows through them very gently. They can be smaller, though, and this forces the water through at slightly higher pressure for more animated effects.

Jets are more spectacular because they shoot water into the air. The most famous uses of jets are in the historic Moorish gardens of Spain. These landscapes feature long, narrow pools that are very similar to our contemporary lap pools. At regular intervals along the edge are small jets that shoot up and into the pool from opposing directions. This is proving to be an excellent way to transform a lap pool into one that is aesthetically important, with the flick of a switch. When the tile and plaster color is properly coordinated, this exercise pool doubles as a romantic vestige of Islamic paradise.

Old Pool Facelifts

In many of today's housing markets the property values have far exceeded the quality of existing old pools. Homeowners are faced with the dilemma of how to renovate their pools from a tired 1960s style to one in keeping with the upgraded house and interior landscape. The good news is that pools can also be remodeled, which is a far more affordable alternative to demolishing the old one to build a new one.

There are different degrees of renovation. You can simply replace the old, worn-out decking with new materials. Removing the vintage coping units to replace them with a solid-pour cantilevered concrete deck is a huge improvement without ever touching the shell of the pool. You can also replace the waterline tile with something more trendy, such as a cutting-edge iridescent tile. Plaster color can also be changed, and a dark bottom may be made white and vice versa.

Critical Codes and Restrictions

Your city will view your new pool installation as a major construction project, and will require the same kind of permits as they do for house remodeling. An abundance of codes and restrictions govern where you may or may not build your pool. Fortunately, pool contractors are well versed in these regulations and will help you identify and work with any that may influence your project.

Each city or county building code is a little bit different, but the single most important concern for your pool location is *setbacks*. A setback ordinance governs how close to the property line you can build a pool or other permanent structure. In some neighborhoods the setback is as little as 3 feet (about 91 cm), but elsewhere it can be two or three times this distance. In some newer planned communities with backyards adjacent to open spaces and common areas, setbacks can be a whopping 25 feet (about 8 m)! Clearly it is essential to verify setbacks before you and your designer decide on a pool location.

Because a pool is excavated, there are also some potential conflicts with utility easements. An *easement* is land you may own, but it remains under the control of the city or utility company. Most utility easements state that there may be no permanent construction within the easement area in order to avoid future conflicts with either overhead wires or underground conduit.

Easements exist in all shapes and sizes. Some may be isolated strips, or large-scale swaths that run through an entire block. There may be actual utilities in that area, or it may simply be reserved for future use. Sometimes easements in very old neighborhoods were created for railroads, for example, which are no longer relevant. In such a case it pays to challenge the city and have an outdated easement removed from your deed so that you can reclaim the space.

You will find easement and sometimes setback requirements recorded on the deed to your property, but a more detailed record is on file with the city or county offices. Do not trust your copy of the deed, because

older properties may have long-forgotten easements, and these may
involve abandoned underground storm drains and other obstacles to excavation of a swimming pool.

Safety Fence Dilemmas

Requisite safety fencing is at once a lifesaving requirement and a serious
aesthetic problem. The rules concerning the fence and its components will
vary from state to state, but all are designed to keep children from drowning in your pool. In general, most safety fence requirements involve two
components: fence height and the gates. In general, fence requirements
range from 4 to 6 feet (about 1 to 2 m) tall, and there must be no gaps
wider than 6 inches (15 cm). The gates must be spring-loaded to automatically close and latch on their own.

Safety fences are required on all pools. For many homeowners, the
perimeter fence of their backyard fulfills these requirements with addition
of spring-loaded gates in the side yard. This allows the pool to exist free
of enclosure within your backyard. But homeowners who have small children or plan to have children in the future often choose to install a safety
fence anyway.

The best solution is to design the landscape so it can evolve with the
family. When the children grow beyond the age where there is risk of
drowning, the safety fence can be removed. If you plan for this at the time

you construct the new fence, your contractor can install it in a way that makes it much easier to remove without damage to the paving and landscape.

Even though lightweight aluminum safety fencing is more expensive than older tubular steel, it is proving worthwhile because it does not stain paving with rust. The fence may be constructed with individual panels, their posts set into sleeves embedded in the paving. In just a few hours' time, part or all of the fence may be removed for special occasions, such as parties. When the event is over the fence is just as easily reinstalled, and when the kids grow up it is easily removed altogether.

Plants: Problems and Problem-Solvers

There is a love–hate relationship between pools and plants. Pools love to be surrounded by a beautiful setting that enhances their natural beauty, but they hate the litter that plants produce. Litter not only makes the pool look bad, it interferes with water quality and clogs the filtration system.

The planted landscape becomes the vital framework that gives a pool character and brings out its best features. Planting is what makes the pool part of the landscape rather than merely a water-filled extension of a patio. Planting around a pool also reflects on the water surface to magnify or compound its presence. Maintenance considerations should not force pools into a barren wasteland when the solution is to find the right plants and put them in the right places.

Understanding the Issues

There are some specifics that must be understood before you consider planting around a pool. First, it is the trees that are the major offenders, although shrubs and vines can present similar problems. Trees shed leaves, flowers, and fruit or seed into pools near or beneath them. Whenever possible, trees should be placed downwind from the pool so that the litter is driven away from the water rather than into it.

Planting evergreens instead of deciduous plants is not the panacea many believe it to be. This is because some evergreens actually shed leaves or needles all year around. Deciduous trees may seem unsuitable, but they shed heavily in just one season, and may be problematic only a month or two out of the year.

Leaf type and shape also influence suitability. It's much easier to get big leathery leaves out of a swimming pool because they remain intact under water for a very long time. Examples of these leaves are those of southern magnolia (*Magnolia grandiflora*) and the rustyleaf fig (*Ficus rubiginosa*). Trees with leaves that are compound and fragile tend to disintegrate into pieces too small to remove without a vacuum. Examples are honeylocust (*Gleditzia triacanthos*) and California pepper (*Schinus molle*). This is also true of conifers, trees that bear needlelike leaves. Thin needles of pines and their ilk are impossible to get off the bottom of the pool without a vacuum.

Flowers can also be difficult, particularly when they are small. Trees with a big seasonal display of flowers with small parts, such as a flowering crabapple (*Malus floribunda*), rain fine petals into the pool. Like those fine compound leaves, these are tough to get out compared to the blossoms of saucer magnolia (*Magnolia solangiana*). Trees like the crabapple, or any other stone fruit, are problematic when located upwind from the pool.

Fruit, no matter how small, may stain not only paving, but pool plaster. Small purple berries of trees and shrubs such as privet contain potent coloring that will stain the pool bottom if left in the pool too long. But the biggest issue is fruit stains on the pool deck. This is compounded by birds, which often come to feed on the fruit. Though many of us love to find wildlife in the landscape, their excreta will further the staining. Larger fleshy fruit can become slippery, too, particularly when wet.

Don't forget that swimming pool users are usually barefoot and dressed in skimpy suits. Plants that bear thorns, such as roses; or those with sharp leaves, like some yuccas and holly, can be painful if someone slips and falls into them. Those plants that draw wasps, bees, and yellowjackets are equally undesirable, particularly if you or anyone in your family is allergic to their stings.

Poolside Landscaping: First, Solve the Problems

All planting design begins by addressing the problems of the pool area to make it more beautiful and conducive to outdoor living. There are a number of conditions shared by most backyard pool areas, because the people who use these spaces do so in a similar way. In the process of landscaping a pool area, it is these concerns that must be addressed first, and then you may design the remainder of the area.

Shade. Shade is among the most important needs for pool areas. Although you want the pool itself to be in the sun for as many hours per day as possible, you probably won't be in it nearly that long. There must be shaded places around the pool for comfortable outdoor living, using trees or other kinds of structures.

Remember that shade trees cast a shadow that extends a long way from the trunk. To avoid casting shadows on the pool, try to locate your shaded living spaces on the north side of the pool, provided this is logical in terms of your house location. The exception to this rule is in very hot climates, such as Arizona. There temperatures can soar in the summer to such extremes that you'll actually need to shade at least part of the pool just to enjoy it in the late afternoon.

ABOVE LEFT, This white structure provides plenty of shade at poolside without any maintenance concerns. ABOVE RIGHT, Landscaping and blue stone link this house to the pool. Large umbrellas provide shade when you want it, then fold up neatly for morning coffee on a sun-drenched terrace. AT LEFT, This older pool area required more shade, so this new prefabricated iron gazebo was erected for instant comfort and maximum interest without burdensome construction.

Man-made shade structures are much quicker to become effective and do not cast such an enormous shadow. That provides greater latitude in where you put them relative to pool exposure. Shade arbors using beams and vines or lattice are great choices that are easy to build, but their location is final. Large canvas market umbrellas can be over 12 feet (about 4 m) in diameter. They prove to be the perfect solution for many pool owners because the umbrella can be moved around from one place to another at will. This is particularly valuable because the position of the sun changes over the course of a day, and you may move the umbrella accordingly. This is also the case with seasonal changes, when the sun's position can be much farther north or south. Either way, by day or by season, umbrellas provide precision shade wherever and whenever you need it.

Privacy. Most people don't want to feel like they live in a fish bowl. Hedges of evergreen trees and shrubs are ideal for raising the visual screening ability of wood fences limited by building codes to just 6 feet (2 m) tall or so. Hedges also disguise a metal safety fence as the plants grow into and surround it. Privacy screens can apply to the whole yard, or to just the pool area specifically, or to just a small part of the pool area that is overexposed. When choosing plants for privacy screens, remember to avoid plants with thorns, berries, and any unnecessary litter problems.

Reliable Evergreen Hedge Screens for Privacy

Botanical Name	Common Name	USDA Climate Zone
Cupressus sempervirens	Italian cypress	7
Escallonia fradesi	Escallonia	7
Euonymus japonicus	Japanese euonymus	5
Fatsia japonica	Japanese aralia	7
Ilex aquifolium	English holly (female)	6
Juniperus chinensis torulosa	Hollywood juniper	4
Laurus nobilis	Sweet bay	8
Podocarpus macrophyllus	Yew pine	9
Prunus laurocerasus	English laurel	6
Sequoia sempervirens	Coast redwood	7
Taxus baccata	English yew	5
Xylosma congestum	Xylosma	9

Glare. Glare is a perennial problem around pools. Sunlight glinting off the water is hard on the eyes during very bright days. Combine that with the glare of white or light gray paving, and the whole area becomes incredibly hostile to the human eye. The green leaves of plants are the most powerful force for cutting glare because they absorb light. The more planting there is around the pool, the more comfortable the area will be as an outdoor living space on hot summer days.

Downplay Security Fencing. Disguise it with foliage and flowers. You can achieve this by draping the fence with beautiful flowering vines or climbing roses to turn a liability into a floral amenity.

Lack of Planting Areas. Where soil is absent, set pots to create a high-profile landscape. Great terra-cotta pots and other unique containers make it possible to bring accent trees, such as flowering crape myrtle or perhaps a fragrant dwarf citrus, into a wholly paved area. They allow you to plant exotic tropicals too tender for your climate zone. Portable pots may be moved under cover for winter, so there is no reason to live amidst a desert when you can create a potted garden of foliage and flowers.

Flowering Background Shrubs*

Botanical Name	Common Name	Evergreen?	USDA Climate Zone
Hibiscus rosa-sinensis	Tropical hibiscus	Yes	10
Hibiscus syriacus	Rose of sharon	No	5
Lagerstroemia indica	Dwarf crape myrtle	No	7
Ligustrum texanum	Texas privet	Yes	7
Nerium oleander	Oleander	Yes	8
Photinia fraseri	Toyon	Yes	7

* These shrubs are high profile with low care and little litter.

Poolside Perennial Color**

Botanical Name	Common Name	USDA Climate Zone
Agapanthus africanus	Lily of the Nile	6
Armeria meritima	Thrift	4
Hemerocallis hybrids	Daylily	5
Iris spp.	Iris	Varies
Lavandula spp.	Lavender	5

** These plants take heat and glare in stride.

Poolside Landscaping: Second, Look for Opportunities

Each swimming pool setting is different, and opportunities to make yours distinctive are all around you. What sets it all off is using plants that add unique qualities of texture and color amidst more standard green foliage. Often these contrasts are what make a garden seem lively, and contributes to an indescribable dynamic.

The unique Tropicanna canna is grown not so much for its vivid orange flowers as for the large, flat leaves striped in distinctive colorful veins. Using this to call attention to points in the landscape is a valuable tool for controlling how a person views your pool-to-garden relationship.

Another distinctive plant is bamboo, and today there are surprisingly cold-hardy species on the market. These plants are both contemporary and

Asian in character, and over time you can prune them to reveal the canes more clearly. They also serve as great screening material that offers fast growth, easy care, limited litter, and a most unique texture. Use to fill a corner, to disguise a second story next door, or to provide background for a Japanese garden lantern or other kinds of sculpture.

The ornamental grasses are great choices, particularly for naturalistic plantings, although they have also been used quite effectively in formal and traditional settings. Use their color and texture, or enjoy the animated flower heads as they nod in the slightest breeze. There is nothing quite like the ruffling of grasses that can be so like the effects of wind on water.

Set it all ablaze with some fiery-hued foliage plants. The gorgeous purple foliage of smoke tree (*Cotinus coggygria* 'Royal Purple') is vivid all season long, then accented with smoke-like puffs of flowers. These are the latest cut flowers of trendy 5th Avenue florists. Or indulge in the seasonal autumn beauty of burning bush (*Euonymus alatus*), which is unmatched in hue and remarkably cold-hardy.

Throughout this book we will challenge your notions of what plants belong around your pool. Explore new compositions for this water-filled landscape that is like no other garden type. For while you spend your days there gliding through the water or lounging in the warmth of the sun, you will drink in a visual feast that will never leave you wanting.

Tropicanna canna features exotic striped foliage and vivid orange flowers.

Living in the Fluid Environment

A swimming pool can be the most rewarding amenity you add to your home. You may find that a preexisting pool needs a contemporary facelift; it can be transformed from a cookie-cutter design into something unique by doing nothing more than changing coping or waterline tile. With a new pool, the only thing that will limit the possibilities is your budget and imagination. Strive for the unique and wonderful in terms of shape and materials. Explore mood-changing options that evoke a particular response, which can be enhanced by well-coordinated landscape planting. Your pool will be, above all, beautiful and will be the undeniable focal point of the entire landscape even after dark.

A swimming pool will serve your family well throughout its life span and offer solutions for changing needs: children enjoy its fun-filled recreation; adults can unwind in the water after a hard day; seniors find exercising in it therapeutic in helping to retain flexibility and strength.

THE SPA

SINCE ANCIENT TIMES it has been called "taking the waters," a means of healing aging bones and tired muscles. Throughout the world, the afflicted flocked to places where hot springs gushed naturally out of the ground. By the Middle Ages towns had sprung up around hot springs, and one Belgian town was named Spa, derived from the Latin *sparsa*, or "to bubble up." Thus the name has come to describe any place where one can take the waters or find remedies.

It was not until the 1820s that Austrian healer Vincenz Priessnitz studied ways to integrate the therapeutic use of hot bubbling water into modern medicine. Since then the use of hot springs in Europe, America, and even Japan has become an accepted treatment for a variety of musculoskeletal problems, as well as such disorders as high blood pressure and eczema. Those with arthritis and chronic bone and joint pain find hydrotherapy the most helpful long-term means of coping with the effects of an incurable condition.

While once it was necessary to travel to a resort for hydrotherapy, advances in the construction of spas for home use have made them a lot more affordable. This flourishing market gave birth to the idea of spas as a social amenity that allows couples or groups to indulge in the comforts of warm water together. Whether social or therapeutic, this kind of water feature works hard to improve the quality of everyday life at home.

There are two basic types of spas commonly used today. First is the *in-ground spa*, built the same way as a swimming pool with a thick concrete shell. This is a permanent spa and can be very expensive to install. It may be constructed independently or integrated into a swimming pool–spa combination. Either way, building a spa is a major project that requires excavation, concrete and steel, and plumbing and mechanical work. Once installed, it remains a permanent part of the yard.

The second, and more widely used, category of spas is called the *portable spa*. This is a wholly manufactured "plug-and-play" version of what is otherwise a costly, permanent, and expensive proposal. These units come fully self-contained, with a molded fiberglass shell that holds the water. These shells are shaped for creative opportunities for seating and may provide better therapeutic posture for the user. This rests within a wood box, and between the two are the plumbing, mechanical apparatuses, and insulation.

Sizes can range from a small unit that suits one or two people to party spas that will seat about eight comfortably. You can choose your fiberglass color and the finish for the exterior woodwork. You'll also find different options for jets and other unique features depending on the manufacturer.

You can place this kind of spa unit anywhere that will support its weight and has access to a power supply. These spas are considered more economical to keep hot than

in-ground spas. The combination of internal insulation and tight-fitting covers reduces heat loss from the water surface. These units range from as little as about $1,000 to deluxe full-sized spas with special features at about three times that price.

A third type of spa, often called *swim-spa,* is less common but solves some very challenging problems. It is hybrid between a pool and spa that allows the user to swim for exercise without a long lane. The unit produces a strong flow of water from one end of the swim-spa, and you swim against it for a vigorous workout suitable for even competitive training. The flow rate is variable, allowing you to swim at the rate you feel the most comfortable.

A swim-spa is expensive, whether you build it as a traditional in-ground unit or install it as a molded fiberglass shell. Despite its versatility, this kind of spa is not widely used because it is so costly to install. It serves a valuable purpose in spatially challenged upscale homes where the need for exercise outweighs the cost.

Homesite Relationships

The spa, because of its therapeutic and social values, fills a slightly different role in the landscape than a swimming pool. Spas are rarely the focal point of a landscape, because their use is more intimate. While a swimming pool is directly related to patios and living spaces indoors and out, the spa is more closely related to the master bedroom.

Patterns of spa users are different than those of swimming pool users. The pool is active during the warmer part of the year, but may sit idle through the remaining colder months. Spas tend to be used all year-round,

and use may actually increase in the winter. In fact, at ski resorts, spas are a major feature of both homes and hotels because skiers appreciate the hydrotherapy benefits after a long, strenuous day on the slopes. Closer to home, hydrotherapy is in higher demand in cold weather, which can stiffen joints and muscles.

The time of day when spas are used also differs from pools. The most active time for spas is directly after work in the evening, when users like to unwind after a hectic day at the office. A spa may also help muscles relax after sitting or standing for too many hours. Later in the evening, some people use their spa just before bed to loosen up for a deeper, more comfortable sleep.

In any case, people most often enter their spa directly from the master bedroom, and return via the same path for a shower. This is why there is such a vital connection between the bedroom or bath and spa. This connection should also be efficient, because a longer walk on a cold night will be increasingly uncomfortable in the winter. It should also be well planned so it is easy to negotiate barefoot, without any tricky stepping stones or unexpected changes in grade.

Another issue to consider is privacy, because spas are a very intimate environment for couples. Many people enjoy using their spa in the nude within the privacy of their own backyard. This means that the spa area should be located with respect to the views from windows of the neighboring houses or adjacent public space. You may want separation from the rest of the backyard landscape as well. The bedroom-to-spa connection may also require additional screening, although this is of secondary importance.

Portable Spa in Your Landscape

The portable spa shares the same master bedroom relationship and accessibility as the in-ground spa. Ease of use in inclement weather and a safe path in and out of the house are essential.

Portable spas are not particularly attractive, no matter how well made. They are essentially a big box on the patio that serves a social or therapeutic purpose, but they're not something we enjoy looking at. Therefore,

The portable spa should appear as an integral part of the landscape, not an afterthought. This design tucks the spa up against the fence line in a convenient but secondary position so that it supports the beauty of the garden. There is a tendency to consider this type of spa the focal point of a space, when it is in reality not an aesthetically appealing feature and should be disguised.

When in a spa, you will have the opportunity to study the tile very closely. This tiny mosaic in Dutch blue is well coordinated with the plaster color and cloaks the dividing wall between spa and pool.

while the aim is to punch up the visibility of an in-ground spa, we want to play down the presence of a portable spa so that it produces as little impact on the surrounding spaces as possible.

Most people try to push the spa into a corner or nook in the landscape where it is out of the way. Positions will be somewhat limited by accessibility because the entire spa must be moved as a single unit. Less visible side yard spaces make some of the best portable spa locations because the house and a solid perimeter fence can provide privacy on two sides.

Many portable spa companies offer wood gazebolike structures that are perfectly designed to accommodate their products. These are desirable if you want protection from the elements while using the spa. In rainy climates, such as the Pacific Northwest, this is a very helpful amenity that will also keep the top of the spa free of heavy snow for ease of use and accessibility. These are structures, however, and in many neighborhoods they may prove to be a serious limitation on where you may put your spa. Building codes and setbacks can preclude the gazebos from side yards, or you may have to keep clear of other property line setbacks. Without the gazebo, you have freedom to place the spa wherever you wish.

Portable spas should be located on a solid, level surface that ensures you can safely enter and exit the water. Spas often end up on wood decks, but a deck must be structurally adequate to withstand the weight of the spa, water, and bodies. Dry rot or undersized beams may make a preexisting deck unstable under the load. Many people set their spa on concrete patios or pour a whole new slab for it. Slabs keep the wood and mechanical apparatuses free of mud, dry rot, and termites to extend the lifespan of the unit. You should not place the spa on bare earth, because it will expand and contract with the seasons, forcing the spa out of level. Earth and dampness can also speed up corrosion on plumbing and electrical work.

A portable spa will benefit from privacy and some degree of separation from more active living spaces. Keep in mind that a portable spa is usually only about 3 to 4 feet (about 1 m) high, so there is no need to disguise it with screening any higher unless you desire more privacy. Many people enjoy looking out onto the garden while using the spa rather than the limited view of an enclosure.

Planting spaces around the edges of a spa allow you to nestle it into the environment. Perennials—particularly those with bladelike foliage, such as daylilies—

OVERHEAD SCREENING

FOR PROBLEMATIC CITY homes, real privacy issues stem from multistory buildings adjacent to your yard. There's no way to keep third- and fourth-floor windows from looking into your private sanctuary. The best solution is to construct an arbor or gazebolike structure over your spa area so that it interferes with the downward view. A structure also provides the opportunity to mount lighting, fans, a mist system, or even stereo speakers overhead to enhance the environment while solving a problem.

are ideal and will not crowd the spa like woody shrubs do over time. Hedges are useful, though, as are dwarf shrubs that grow about as high as the spa walls. The idea is to retain accessibility to the spa but screen its presence out of the landscape when it is not in use.

Exploiting In-Ground Options

The in-ground spa can be created in a myriad of shapes and sizes, while the portable spa limits you to those offered by the manufacturer. In-ground spa construction utilizes the same materials as a swimming pool, sharing many of the same options. There are choices of materials for decking, accent coping, waterline tile, and plaster color. Because it is smaller than a pool, you will want to make bold choices that stand out as a creative, artistic feature rather than sticking with a default standard.

If the spa is to be a visual feature, which is often the case in smaller gardens, take advantage of high-quality materials. Smaller yards require less material, which may allow you to upgrade more economically than you think. Rather than concrete, use the upscale veneers and tile options featured in Chapter 6. You'll also find some formal fountain ideas in Chapter 4.

The edges of this spa are raised just a few inches above the surrounding patio. This technique adds interest and also serves as a safety feature that protects against a pedestrian accidentally stepping into the spa.

ABOVE LEFT, When the
spa is elevated above
the pool, additional
engineering is required
on the face of exposed
outside walls.
ABOVE RIGHT, You can
explore unusual
materials that make
the division between
pool and spa appear
more natural and less
dependent on tile.

While sitting in the spa you will have a much more intimate view of the waterline tile, and here you can explore iridescent tiles that give the perception of greater depth. Mottling and irregular surfaces on the tile make light play on them differently. Don't hesitate to consider luscious Spanish tile if it is compatible with your whole landscape color scheme. Try two colors of tile arranged in bands or vertical stripes, and other creative combinations. You might even try making intricate patterns inspired by Spanish mosaics.

The color of the spa plaster is as important here as it is in a swimming pool. A light plaster will be more fully illuminated at night, which is great to enjoy as a nighttime focal point—but it is rather revealing to less than fully clad users. The turquoise spa is a fresh and bright element in small gardens.

Many homeowners choose dark-plaster spas for a variety of reasons. Dark plaster is more energy efficient because it enjoys passive solar heating benefits. This plaster type is more natural and moody and contributes to more of a fantasy character than brighter spas. The surrounding land-

scape of ambient lighting is far better enhanced by the muted light of a dark spa at night.

The in-ground spa can be constructed at whatever size and shape you wish, but always remember that the larger the body of water, the more it will cost to both build and heat. The majority of in-ground spas tend to be round, square, or hexagonal in shape, but don't let this stop you from exploring more innovative shapes. If you are using the spa for particular types of physical therapy, be sure your contractor knows these needs to ensure that the positioning of jets in the spa conforms to your needs.

Some spas are created to appear more naturalistic. They often include the integration of boulders, waterfalls, and appropriate planting to appear more like a natural hot spring. In fact, this is nature's choice of hot spring design, and it touches a primal chord in all of us. Irregular shapes with nooks and crannies provide lots of opportunities for creation of adjacent planting, making a natural, private, relaxing sanctuary. Try to coordinate plaster color so it will blend naturally if rocks or boulders are integrated into the pool.

Dark plaster and natural rockwork define this spa located in the upper pool. This free-form shape requires more attention to detail than the typical square, round, and hexagonal spas.

MANIFEST ELEGANCE
Design by Michael Glassman

DESIGN OF ANY environment is a creative act that blends a strong sense of beauty with the cold, hard calculation of the builder. No design occurs in a vacuum, but is achieved by the synthesis of desires and constraints to produce a space that is wholly responsive to the site and its user.

EVERYTHING THAT IS BEAUTIFUL AND NOBLE IS THE PRODUCT OF REASON AND CALCULATION.
—CHARLES BAUDELAIRE, *SELECTED WRITINGS ON ART AND ARTISTS*, 1972

Although the lots in this suburban community were quite large, the front yard setback requirements left very little space in the back for outdoor living. What did exist in this homesite was an L-shaped backyard with about 50 percent of the space on one side of the house. The challenge was to create a high-quality environment for the owners that was as luxurious as the inside of the newly remodeled and upgraded house.

There was little that Michael Glassman could salvage when he first encountered the yard, which featured a cracked concrete pool deck. Just a few feet from the back door was a wholly unsafe spa that not only dominated what little space there was, it was an accident waiting to happen. It is never a good idea to place a potential hazard so close to a doorway.

Just beyond that lay an outdated swimming pool that consumed what little area was left, save a narrow planting strip along the rear perimeter of the lot. The side yard was not visible from the main living rooms of the house and was not part of the pool area per se.

Michael first eliminated the old spa entirely to reclaim every bit of backyard patio space he could muster. He created a whole new spa tucked back into the corner beside the master bedroom for more convenient access. This was surrounded by a low wall on two sides, which allowed the planting behind to be raised up and provide maximum screening without using oppressive hedge plants. In association with the wall he created a waterfall into the spa capable of drowning out both household and city noises.

The pool received a makeover, with new streamlined slate coping and plaster color more in keeping with the color palette of the house and adjacent patio. Without the old spa taking up space, the house and pool connection now featured the luxury of an open slate-covered deck. Indian slate is the integrating component of the entire pool–spa–patio area, bringing all the separate components together with a single rich material.

OPPOSITE, This spa is tucked away in the corner of an expansive landscape. It is an integral part of the entire space and adds interest through this fountain built into a retaining wall for enclosure and privacy.

ABOVE LEFT, The spa had
originally been located to
the left in the center of
the patio area. The new
location allowed this
entire space to become
usable and made the
sharp lines of the pool
more dramatic. ABOVE
RIGHT, This is a spatially
economical water feature
that does not require an
upper pool. When not
operating, it is practically
invisible, but when
flowing it provides a
means of drowning out
surrounding city noise.

A large amount of the lot's backyard area was tucked into the far corner
situated at the apex of the L shape. It is here that sufficient space existed to
create an elaborate outdoor room covered by an open-beam arbor and
surrounded by low walls. It was outfitted with the most popular, cutting-edge
amenities, including a cook center and countertop. There was also a state-of-
the-art gas grill and sink, with a small refrigerator tucked in underneath.

Other elements helped make the space comfortable in extremes of weather.
To warm the area on cool days or chilly nights, an outdoor fireplace hearth
burns firewood or a gas fire. In the heat of summer, an overhead arbor draped
in vines provides welcome shade, but allows plenty of light through to ensure
it is not too dark. The back margins of this space are densely planted so that
over time there will be no view of the rear fence remaining.

The corner outdoor kitchen space looks out onto the side yard garden, which
is a wholly different experience. This is a sun-filled open garden, semiformal
and nicely symmetrical. It is centered on a rectangular pool with a single-tier
"birdbath" fountain. A young boxwood hedge and blooming seasonal color
surround the water feature. Rather than continue the darker paving, Michael
chose a more Old World decomposed granite surfacing, with pale coloring to
create a high-contrast frame for the darker tones of the slate water feature.

The center of the garden is framed in banks of roses, both shrub and tree
forms, new tea roses, and charming old-fashioned varieties in a diversity of
colors. Along the building and fence lines are trellis panels to support the

ABOVE LEFT, The water of
spa and pool meet in this
precise channel that spans
the dividing bond beam.
ABOVE RIGHT, Tucked into
the corner of the
landscape is an outdoor
kitchen and entertainment
area. It is protected from
the summer sun by a vine-
shrouded arbor, which
allows some light through
and is less visually
oppressive than a solid
cover. AT LEFT, This living
space is warm and cozy
on days a bit too chilly to
spend time outdoors. A
gas fireplace also burns
wood and offers cheerful
warmth and an attractive
back wall for an intimate
garden room.

young, fragrant jasmine vines. Beneath them are beds of perennials and dwarf shrubs that will eventually mature to make these fences disappear into the background as well.

This landscape is a remarkable example of how a noble, timeless design can be created around an old, worn-out swimming pool. Through meticulous calculation, not one inch of this city lot was left out of the design. It is a beautiful combination of three distinct areas: an active pool and spa, an outdoor entertainment center, and a passive fountain-centered contemplative flower garden.

What we learn from the incalculable effort is that water works even in the most challenging spaces. It also shows how the manipulation of water and water features can both solve problems and enhance daily living. Old pools can become new again. Overexposed spas can be moved to a more intimate setting. Even rose gardens may become filled with birds and glistening water with a simple but elegant fountain.

Creating an Experience

The well-designed spa is more than a functional part of the landscape—it is the central element of an environmental experience. This space must appeal to you in many ways, because you spend so much time there passively observing the surroundings. Attention to detail is also very important, because everything is viewed up close. Beauty is paramount so that the environment is visually pleasing day and night. All of this hinges on the surrounding landscape and the plants used to support the overall concept.

A private spa enclosure can easily be added to a more exposed side of the house with a screen fence draped in fragrant vines.

The spaces around your spa will be intimate, so it is vital that the plants chosen be smaller in scale to fill in the gaps between larger trees and shrubs in the background. Otherwise, when in the water you are gazing out onto bare dirt at eye level. Always remember that whatever you choose must look great under close scrutiny at the eye level of a spa user.

The primary need that will drive how this environment is created will be privacy. That is usually contingent on some sort of enclosure, but you want be sure that it is accomplished in a way that does not overpower the space. Fences are the most efficient means of immediate enclosure where space is limited. In more expansive areas, a diverse planting of trees, shrubs, and perennials will, over time, provide a dense and very attractive perimeter.

Solid enclosures, such as fences and walls, have two liabilities: they block the exchange of both light and air. With the heat of the spa, you will want air circulation to ensure a pleasant experience in warmer weather. The best enclosures are composed of semitransparent screen fences, with economical wood lattice favored for blocking views without sacrificing too much light or air.

The size of the openings in prefabricated lattice panels will vary. The smaller the opening, the more privacy you will have right away. Panels are also available with openings considerably larger, and though these sacrifice privacy at first, the integration of vines into the open lattice increases the density of the enclosure over time. Many prefer to wait for the beautiful foliage and flowers of vines to mature rather than living with a denser screen. In fact, the lattice will disappear altogether beneath the vines so that ultimately you will be surrounded by a wall of leafy plants.

Vines used on spa enclosures must be carefully chosen to fit the space and to do the job required. Some vines are not particularly dense, such as

clematis, so be aware that you may need more individuals to provide the
screening you have in mind. On the other hand, vines like Japanese honeysuckle can completely take over in just a few seasons. Evergreen vines
will provide year-round screening, but these are usually limited to warmer
climates.

The vine must also remain in scale with the space, because a large, ram-
pant grower, such as wisteria, can turn into a maintenance problem requiring frequent pruning during the growing season. However, if you're
looking for fast coverage of an overhead shade arbor, either to get users
out of the sun or to block views from windows up above, these big, vigorous plants are the best choice. The best candidates for this purpose, all
hardy to Zone 5, are wisteria (*Wisteria floribunda*); scarlet trumpet vine
(*Campsis radicans*); seedless grapes (*Vitis vinifera*); and Hall's Japanese honeysuckle (*Lonicera japonica* 'Halliana').

If you plan to use vines with scented flowers, be sure to find a fra-
grance you enjoy. Mature jasmine vines can be quite overwhelming when
in bloom within small spaces, which may be fragrant to some while nox-
ious to others.

Although there are many vines to choose from, there are only a few
that not only are reliable growers and reasonably well-behaved, but will
remain in scale with the average spa environment. These are also good

choices for disguising swimming pool safety fences under a cloak of attractive foliage and flowers.

Carolina Jessamine (*Gelsemium sempervirens*)

This glossy-leaf evergreen is from the southeastern United States and retains all the pest and disease resistance typical of native plants. It offers year-round screening topped off by a cascade of bright yellow, fragrant, trumpet-shaped flowers in spring. Even when not in bloom, its cascade-like growth habit drapes beautifully over solid fences and walls. It is the best vine for shrouding chain link fences. Cold-hardy to Zone 7.

Blue Passion Flower (*Passiflora caerulea*)

No other vine conveys such an exotic tropical character as the passion flower, and this species is hardier than most. While it remains evergreen in warmer climates, it will lose its leaves where it is colder. Plants grow quickly, cover well, and climb with corkscrew tendrils that grab the trellis rather than draping or twining like other vines. The intricate beauty of the flower is so remarkably detailed that it is a visual feast to enjoy up close while relaxing in your spa. Cold-hardy to Zone 8.

Jasmine

There are actually two species of jasmine grown today that are relatively hardy and bear the intensely scented flowers so beloved by gardeners. The vines are fine-branching, and therefore easily woven into lattice, even when the holes are on the small side. Common white jasmine (*Jasminum officinale*) is hardy to Zone 7. It will be deciduous where winters are colder, but it will remain evergreen if not exposed to frost. Slightly more tender is *Jasminum polyanthum*, a vine widely planted in California and across the southern states. Hardy to Zone 8, it remains evergreen and blooms abundantly over a long season in spring and early summer. Both of these vines are powerful aromatherapy tools.

Virginia Creeper (*Parthenocissus qinquefolia*)

This vine does not flower but is every bit as showy as the others. It is native to the northeastern United States, and is self-clinging by means of suction-cup holdfasts that are gentle on masonry. This vine offers a different character in every season, but provides little screening in winter when leafless. Spring buds burst into lime green five-part leaves that darken to emerald over summer, and then change to fiery red for an autumn show. It's a cousin to Boston ivy (*Parthenocissus tricuspidata*), which clings more tightly to surfaces and bears a smaller three-part leaf. Both are deciduous and hardy to Zone 4.

Purple-Leaf Japanese Honeysuckle (*Lonicera japonica* 'Purpurea')

The honeysuckle is perhaps our most widely recognized flowering vine, but it is too large for most tight settings. However, this cultivar is not only smaller but better-behaved and more attractive. Its flowers are a luscious purple-red and a big draw for hummingbirds. Blossoms are as fragrant as the standard honeysuckle, with a bonus of slightly plum-tinted leaves. This plant is hardy to Zone 6 and is evergreen, though partially deciduous in colder winters.

Star Jasmine, Confederate Jasmine (*Trachelospermum jasminoides*)

Despite its name, this plant is not related to true jasmine, although it bears equally fragrant flowers. This leathery twining vine is a show-stopper when cloaked in small white, star-shaped blossoms. It is the consummate plant to cloak ugly chain-link or pool safety fencing because it snakes up the bars all by itself. It is somewhat drought-resistant, evergreen, and less frost-hardy to Zone 9.

Ideas for Creating a Fantasy Environment

Your spa can become the fantasy environment of your dreams that allows you to climb inside to leave the world behind. Once you have established your privacy enclosure, the inside may be designed through plants to evoke a beautiful, serene place in nature. The two most popular environments are a tropical paradise and a romantic woodland glade. Each will require a different set of plants, and both can be achieved no matter what climate you live in, save the coldest zones.

A landscaped area is composed of many different kinds of plants, and for spa areas, as already discussed, you will be sitting in the water at ground level, making shorter plants very important. Many of these will be dwarf shrubs, herbaceous perennials, and others, such as ferns and small palms. In addition, it is essential that you choose plants with an idea of their size at maturity. A single overly large shrub can overwhelm a garden, pushing everything else out of the way.

Tropical Paradise

The key to creating a tropical paradise is based on two components: foliage and flowers. Tropical leaves tend to be very large, like those of houseplants, which are actually from tropical environments and cannot grow in the cold outside. The bigger and more interesting the leaves, the more tropical your environment will appear. You can also push the frost line by exploring new ways to look at otherwise common temperate-zone plants.

The second defining element of this environment is flowers, which tend to be large and very bold-colored. Flowers can be produced on perennials, as well as shrubs, vines, and some small trees. Hot colors provide a warm-climate feeling, so emphasize bold flowers in red, orange, magenta, and yellow, with purple and strong blues for accents.

Compositions of plants for a tropical character should be densely planted in order to give that lush, junglelike appearance. Keep the taller plants with big leaves behind the smaller perennials to ensure all are equally visible. Also, plant the perennials in front of woody shrubs in order to cover up any exposed lower branches or stems.

Many tropicals, such as large-leaf caladium, are essential to the jungle garden but won't take a frost. A very similar bear's breech (*Acanthus mollis*) is a perfect alternative and just as tropical-looking, but it will survive winter cold to about 10° F (about 12° C). Though *Acanthus* dies back to the ground, it recovers quickly come spring.

Bamboo is one of the keystone plants of the tropical landscape. Many species are cold-hardy, so don't write it off as an accent or privacy screen until you've checked it out with the garden center.

ABOVE LEFT, The distinctive elephant-ear shape of colocasia combines with palmate castor bean. These are two of the most common tropical-looking foliage plants. ABOVE RIGHT, The Mediterranean *Acanthus mollis* produces large, exotic foliage and tall spiked flowers that may appear tropical but are surprisingly hardy.

Botanical Name	Common Name	Height/Type	USDA Climate Zone
Acanthus mollis	Bear's breech	5' (2 m)/ Perennial	7
Agapanthus africanus	Lily of the Nile	3' (91 cm)/ Perennial	8
Buddleia davidii 'Nanoensis'	Dwarf butterfly bush	5' (2 m)/ Shrub	5
Canna indica 'Phaison'	Tropicanna canna	5' (2 m)/ Perennial	7
Chamerops humilis	Mediterranean fan palm	5' (2 m)/ Palm	9
Clivia miniata	Kaffir lily	2' (61 cm)/ Perennial	10
Cyperus alternifolius	Umbrella plant	4' (1 m)/ Grass	8
Daphne odora 'Aureo-marginata'	Variegated daphne	4' (1 m)/ Shrub	7
Equisetum hyemale	Horsetail reed grass	3' (91 cm)/ Reed	5
Fatsia japonica	Japanese aralia	10' (3 m)/ Shrub	8
Gardenia 'Kleim's Hardy'	Kleim's hardy gardenia	3' (91 cm)/ Shrub	7

Botanical Name	Common Name	Height/Type	USDA Climate Zone
Hemerocallis hybrids	Hardy hybrid daylily	3′ (91 cm)/ Perennial	5
Liriope muscari 'Majestic'	Majestic lilyturf	2′ (61 cm)/ Perennial	6
Moraea bicolor	African iris	3′ (91 cm)/ Perennial	8
Nandina domestica	Heavenly bamboo	6′ (2 m)/ Shrub	6
Nephrolepis exaltata	Sword fern	2′ (61 cm)/ Fern	8
Phyllostachys nigra	Black bamboo	25′ (8 m)/ Grass	7
Pleioblastus variegatus	Dwarf whitestripe bamboo	4′ (1 m)/ Grass	6
Strelitzia reginae	Bird of paradise	4′ (1 m)/ Perennial	10
Tulbaghia violacea	Society garlic	2′ (61 cm)/ Perennial	10
Trachycarus fortunei	Windmill palm	20′ (6 m)/ Palm	8

ABOVE LEFT, It's not necessarily the plants, but how you use them that creates that luscious tropical garden. This Tropicanna canna combined with common purple fountain grass is visually exciting and easy to grow. ABOVE RIGHT, The gorgeous rose mallow (*Hibiscus moscheutos*) is remarkably hardy to Zone 4! Though it dies back in the winter, it can rebound to reach 5 feet (about 2 m) tall and as wide in a single season. It makes an excellent background shrub for cold-challenged fantasy landscapes where tropical hibiscus is out of the question.

TOP LEFT, Even though this beautiful golden elder (*Sambucus nigra* 'Aurea') appears tender, it is incredibly cold-hardy and ideal for planting around spas. It will survive winters to Zone 3 and bears this lovely coloring throughout the year to add light and interest to any woodland setting. TOP RIGHT, Whenever a spa is in the shade of buildings or trees, use variegated plants to create the illusion of more sunlight than really exists. ABOVE LEFT, Japanese painted ferns are tiny members of the woodland garden, but they are absolutely fascinating at eye level when you sit down in the spa. ABOVE RIGHT, There are ferns native to woods from Canada to Mexico, and all are ideal for landscaping a spa garden. These male ferns will reach 4 feet (about 1 m) at maturity, and are perfectly compatible with charming fuchsias.

Woodland Getaway

The woodland setting is comprised of more traditional plants characteristic of the temperate climate zones. There will be a lot more latitude here, as these plants tend to be much more cold-hardy. They are also more recognizable to northern gardeners.

The key players are woody shrubs, ferns, grasses, and sedges, along with a few unusual choices for interest. The colors are not so vivid; flowers are more muted and cool-colored, with emphasis on bright blues and purples. It is difficult to find the heady fragrances of tropical flowers among these more northerly species.

The feathery foliage and delightful flowers of woodland bleeding heart (*Dicentra* 'Luxuriant') are delicate and perfect for close-up inspection while you relax in the warm hot spring.

Botanical Name	Common Name	Height/Type/ Evergreen?	USDA Climate Zone
Acer palmatum	Japanese maple	20' (6 m)/ Tree/No	5
Ajuga reptans	Carpet bugle	12" (30 cm)/ Groundcover/Yes	4
Azalea hybrids	Azaleas	Varies/ Shrub/Varies	Varies
Camellia japonica	Japanese camellia	15'+ (5 m)/ Shrub/Yes	7
Cornus stolonifera	Red twig dogwood	9' (3 m)/ Shrub/No	2
Dryopteris feliz-mas 'Robusta'	Robust male fern	4' (1 m)/ Fern/Yes	4
Hosta hybrids	Plantain lily	2–3' (61–91 cm)/ Perennial/No	3–6
Hydrangea macrophylla	Hydrangea	6–10' (2–3 m)/ Shrub/No	6
Iris siberica	Siberian iris	2' (61 cm)/ Perennial/No	4
Miscanthus sinensis 'Variegatus'	Variegated fountain grass	6' (2 m)/ Grass/No	5
Pennisetum alopecuroides	Fountain grass	3' (91 cm)/ Grass/No	5
Pieris japonica	Andromeda	6' (2 m)/ Shrub/Yes	5
Polystichum setiferum	Alaska fern	3' (91 cm)/ Fern/No	5
Rhododendron hybrids	Rhododendron	Varies/ Shrub/Yes	4–5
Syringa vulgaris hybrids	Common lilac	6–10' (2–3 m)/ Shrub/No	4

Strap-Leafed Perennials

Some of the best plants to explore for spa-related landscaping are loosely grouped according to the shape of their leaves and habit. Many designers call them *strap-leafed plants*, because the long, thin leaves are straplike in form, but their color and texture can change dramatically from one species to another. They are all herbaceous—that is, they lack woody parts, and are classified in the lily, iris, and amaryllis families. Some grow from a bulb or bulbous root structure, or from a group of thick, fleshy roots.

The most important landscape value is that they do not outgrow their space, as woody plants often do. They grow quickly and flower prolifically. The foliage of some is the most desirable quality, particularly those that offer striped or variegated cultivars. The plants with very erect forms provide an attractive reedlike effect that is visually appropriate in conjunction with natural water features.

These are excellent container plants as well as in-ground candidates. A single plant will grow to a larger diameter and bloom more abundantly over just a few years. Older plants may be divided into many new individuals in the dormant season. It is important to know the hardiness of any potential candidate to ensure it will survive through the winter. Those that are hardy usually die back to the ground but regrow vigorously in spring. In warmer climates they may remain evergreen year-round.

Daylily (*Hemerocallis* hybrids)

Daylilies should not be confused with true Asiatic lilies, which are very different plants. Ease of pollination has yielded an astonishing 40,000 named daylily cultivars in a broad range of flower color from red through orange, salmon, and white. There are daylilies that bloom early, midseason, and late, so you can combine them to extend the flowering as long as possible. Some of these are dwarf plants, which are better for containers or to use in smaller gardens. If you live in a colder climate, it is essential that you choose cultivars that are hardy, or they won't survive the winter. Some daylilies can be found that are hardy to Zone 4 (-20° F, -29° C), others take no colder than Zone 5 (-10° F, -23° C). The "evergreen" daylilies will survive only to Zone 7 (0° F, 18° C). Though they die back where there is frost, these evergreens are rugged individuals that will retain their foliage year-round in warmer regions, and are the favorites there.

Iris (*Iris siberica*)

Although there are many species of iris to explore, this one is the best for poolside landscaping. Plants are remarkably cold-hardy to Zone 4, but also produce large clumps of attractive foliage and plentiful flowers. This iris makes a great landscape plant that evokes the feeling of the water garden

flag iris (*Iris pseudoacorus*) in dry ground at poolside. Long, thin upright blades to 2 feet (about 61 cm) tall make Siberian iris a great accent even when not in bloom. A number of cultivars offer different flower colors in shades of blue, white, yellow, lilac, and purple. For smaller gardens, consider miniature bearded iris (*Iris pumila*), which grows just 4 to 6 inches (about 10 to 15 cm) tall. It's a colorful and cold-hardy substitute for its larger Siberian cousins.

Lilyturf (*Liriope muscari*)

These very reliable plants are both attractive accents and problem-solving perennials. Their common name attests to the grasslike foliage and growth habit. They hail from China and have long been a part of traditional Asian gardens. Although plants will bloom with attractive spikes of flowers much like those of the grape hyacinth, this is not their most desirable characteristic. Liriope species are mostly grown for their dark green strap-leafed foliage, with some cultivars offering dramatic creamy variegated foliage, as with striped 'Silvery Sunproof.' Cultivars range in height from about 12″ to 24″ (about 30 to 61 cm) tall and as wide. They are most often used as a dense border to soften the edges of pavement or lawns, but larger plants such as *Liriope gigantia* will reach 3 feet (about 91 cm) with age. The majority of these plants thrive in locations protected from a hot western exposure and are hardy to Zone 6.

Lily of the Nile (*Agapanthus africanus*)

This may be the most frequently used perennial in the warmer parts of America. It's valued for the bright lime green succulent leaves and starburst

ABOVE LEFT, Agapanthus lily is a rare source of blue in gardens that proves both reliable and attractive even when out of bloom. ABOVE RIGHT, The white fortnight lily offers the best sharp, upright foliage, with a bonus of flowers that come alive under a full moon. Sit in the spa by moonlight with the lights off and watch them glow!

of blue flowers atop a long, straight rod that rises 3 feet (about 91 cm) or more above mature plants. It is native to South Africa, not to the Nile region of Egypt. Bright green, succulent leaves produce plants to 4 feet (about 1 m) in height and diameter that remain evergreen year-round. Although plants do take a frost, they are not hardy below Zone 8. New cultivars such as the Headbourne hybrids offer both lighter and darker shades of blue than the original species, plus improved cold-hardiness. There is a dwarf variety, 'Peter Pan,' for smaller spaces.

Fortnight Lily (*Moraea iridioides*)
African Iris (*Moraea bicolor*)

These two closely related species differ only slightly in flower color. They are upright irislike plants hardy to Zone 8; they hail from South Africa, which makes them very drought resistant. For a more traditional white iris flower, choose *M. iridioides*, and for a more tropical-looking flower choose *M. bicolor*. Otherwise, the plants are identical, growing to 3 feet (about 91 cm) and as wide with a deep green coloring. They are easy to care for.

Waterfalls and the Spa

The most popular water feature, in conjunction with spas, is the waterfall. Before adding one to your landscape, it's important that you understand some basics concerning the anatomy of a waterfall and the related hydraulic concepts. Knowing this enables you to better work with your pool contractor to create the best water feature possible, rather than leaving these design choices to him or her.

The single most important consideration in creating a waterfall is elevation. The source of the water must be located at a higher elevation than its final destination. The higher the source, the farther the water falls and the more noise it makes. Getting this source elevated can be problematic on flat or very small sites, and is the single biggest design challenge.

The width of the waterfall is also vital. You can compensate for lack of height by creating a much wider waterfall so that overall there is still the same area of moving water visible. Niagara Falls, which is just 182 feet (about 55 meters) high but extends horizontally for over 1 mile (about 2 km), is recognized around the world for its horizontal distance.

Volume of flow is as important as height and width. There is a direct relationship between the width of your waterfall and the volume of flow that passes over the weir, or spillway. Waterfalls that pass over the spillway in an even sheet require a minimum flow rate to function properly. Too little volume causes the water to flow over in an irregular way, leaving the edges dry and causing a loss of velocity that subjects the falling water to wind and other disturbances. Clearly, success is dependent on a well-engineered ratio of weir width to volume.

Water Curtain

The sheer geometry of a precision waterfall has led designers to call them *water curtains* or *sheetfalls*. These are precisely constructed so that the water flows over the weir in a thin, even sheet that is enhanced by strategic night lighting. Designers often position lights under the water curtain to shine up through its thin sheet, or place lights behind to illuminate it more evenly.

A sheetfall can be created with an open water source or a closed one. The weir and its cantilevered lip may be part of an elevated open pool that is either purely aesthetic or useful as a spa or wading pool. This is the more expensive choice and requires considerably more area to create the upper pool.

The other approach is to hide this source underneath paving or masonry, which is often the only choice where there is simply no room to create the upper pool. It is also less expensive. This technique provides you with a high-profile wall with a wide slot in the face from which the water issues. It's not uncommon to use a panel of translucent glass block built into the wall but behind the sheet of water to provide more dramatic illumination.

The weir for either technique must be perfectly level. Because water finds its own level in accordance with gravity, an out-of-level weir will reveal itself instantly with the majority of the water flowing off the lower side. The weir must be fitted with a cantilevered lip that extends outward at least 1 inch (about 3 cm), but usually more. It is essential, for otherwise the water would simply adhere to the wall and flow down its surface rather than free-falling into the pool below.

Cantilevered lips can be made out of many different materials, depending on the climate and application. Most often chosen are large pieces of tile with rounded edges. Slabs of granite or marble are not uncommon on weirs too wide to use tile. When the weir must be shaped to funnel water better, which is often crucial in windy sites, either stainless steel or specially formed clear plastic are preferred.

There are many variations on design of the water curtain feature that are valuable problem-solvers for landscapes with difficult grades or limited space. The most important part of this water feature is that big visibility can be achieved without sacrificing much area. This taller-than-wide approach is a great device against retaining walls at the back of the yard. On some cut-and-fill homesites, the cut slope comes down into the back-

This water curtain illustrates the kind of precision work necessary to make water sheet off a flat weir in a single unbroken fall. Such work requires a highly skilled designer, contractor, and sometimes even a structural engineer!

yard at a steep 2:1 ratio. This negative is transformed into opportunity when the waterfall is built into the slope to gain more height.

Materials for a curtain waterfall are important not only to its beauty but to its relationship with the surrounding landscape. Whenever possible, be materially consistent throughout the site so that there is a visual link between the house, its interior, and the outside living and landscape spaces. Sitewide continuity ensures the water feature appears appropriate and complementary when nestled within the context of the holistic landscape.

The back wall of the sheetfall is the most visible part of the water feature. You will be able to choose a shiny glazed ceramic tile for a back wall that is easy to care for and highly attractive. That same tile can extend onto the pool steps, at the waterline, and as caps for walls of any height to further integrate the project.

Glass block is one of the most innovative materials found in pool water features today. It serves as a structural unit as well as a dynamic feature for lighting. Glass block that is well illuminated is a valuable and economical way to upgrade an average waterfall. Although you may think that glass block only belongs in modern or deco-style landscapes, it fits beautifully into a wide variety of traditional styles as well. Glass block can also be integrated into freestanding walls elsewhere in the pool area to break up expanses of masonry, or to provide opportunities for lighting in darker places in the landscape.

THEY SAID IT COULDN'T BE DONE
Design by Michael Glassman

THE HOUSE WAS in a great old neighborhood of the city and the owners desperately wanted a pool. Contractors came to look at the tiny backyard and all shook their heads, saying it couldn't be done without cutting down the two old trees that screened off the neighbors' homes. To make matters worse, the detached garage was in the backyard, taking up much more valuable space. When Michael Glassman walked on the job, the clients were preparing to give up hope for a pool, much less the high-profile pool and spa combination they dreamed of.

SO DIFFICULT IS IT TO BRING PEOPLE TO APPROVE OF ANY ALTERATION OF ANCIENT CUSTOMS: THEY ARE ALWAYS NATURALLY DISPOSED TO ADHERE TO OLD PRACTICES, UNLESS EXPERIENCE EVIDENTLY PROVES THEIR INEXPEDIENCY.

—LIVIUS (59 B.C.–17 A.D.)

Michael's solution was to turn the exterior of the garage into a vital part of the pool complex. Where the swimming pool companies saw a hole in the ground surrounded by requisite deck, Michael knew that he could solve the problem by building up, rather than out. He jammed the pool up against the garage and used the building as backing for a beautiful, vertical water feature with planters. This produced enough saved space on the other end of the yard to easily accommodate both the trees and the spa they wanted.

The first step was to disguise the garage by painting the wall a dark color and facing it with a trellis of 12-inch-square (30-cm-square) wood grids painted white for contrast. It was constructed to exact dimensions

This beautiful pool and spa water feature uses the power of symmetry to create a large-scale composition that looks good at any angle.

AT LEFT, This beautiful wall fountain set onto the end of the garage leaves little clue that a purely functional building stands behind. Pushing up against the garage with just 1 inch (about 25 mm) of clear space between the back of the fountain and the stucco building ensures that both of them stand structurally secure. ABOVE, The old Roman pedestal urn helps to enhance the symmetry with understated elegant containers that insert floral accents into the large area of paving and water.

so that nonclinging vines grow right up and onto the peaked roof. Then the water feature itself was centered on the wall with an arched backing of veneer brick and ceramic accent tile.

Although the veneer appears part of the wall, it is actually freestanding just 1 inch (about 25 mm) away from the outer garage wall. This eliminates any risk of moisture passing through the masonry to damage the garage. On either side are two raised planters just 2 feet (about 61 cm) wide, which is all that was needed to adequately frame the fountain and provide places for the vines.

The owners hoped to create a more classical Old World feeling to the space, so they chose a reproduction bronze sculpture of a boy with a lion's head pouring water. This stands amidst a pool of water bounded by brick on the sides and glass block for lighting on the front, topped with cobalt blue waterline tile. It is raised about 2 feet (about 61 cm) above the level of the pool water surface. Although incomparable in daylight, this water feature is even more beautiful at night when hidden lights inside the pool shine out through the block and upward onto the sculpture.

The body of the pool is a classic rectangular Roman shape with bull-nosed brick coping that is integrated into the spa at the far end. The decking was composed of matching brick in a basketweave pattern. The blue tile repeats to unify the fountain, pool, and attached spa. White plaster gives the pool a bright character in such a shaded lot.

Along each of the long pool sides are Moorish jets that shoot out into the center for a second fountain effect. Fiber-optic lights hidden under the coping edge illuminate the waterline tile and make the jets of water more visible at night. The fiber-optic light changes gradually from red to green and back again, although it can be clear white light as well.

Around the edges of the minimal pool deck are low seatwalls of matching brick, which are integral with raised planting areas behind. This is a critical issue because the entire backyard was so poorly drained that it was difficult to grow plants there at all. Elevated planters ensure that the new shrubs and vines will remain healthy.

The existing perimeter fences were upgraded. They were painted a dark color and superimposed with white trellis grids to match those applied to the garage. A wide decorative wood cap finishes the fence tops and provides a perfect place to hide more fiber-optic lighting.

The final solution to this drainage nightmare was to use a narrow area behind the garage as an underground sump. Gravel packed, it will collect

Opposite, This water feature is incredibly detailed, leaving no part undecided. The back wall, with its brick tile details and accent band, blends seamlessly into the nearby system of raised brick planters. The sculpture is perfectly finished to blend into the water. The front face of this upper pool is glass block so that at night the water curtain that flows into the pool is beautifully illuminated. Finally, the owners have carefully arranged vines to nestle the sculpture into the garden setting, making it more integrated with the surrounding landscape.

This kind of small-scale, high-profile water feature requires attention to every detail. Note how the brick cap is cut into small, perfectly aligned mortar joints with mitered corners. The transition from cobalt blue face tile to the brick on the side is so well done you hardly notice the change.

runoff and hold it until the water is naturally absorbed into the subsoil. The pit was 5 feet (about 2 m) square and 6 feet (about 2 m) deep. The water enters this invisible and complex drainage system through open slots in the brick paving. Then it is shunted through a collector pipe that feeds into the sump.

This was a beautiful solution to an impossible backyard challenge. Not only did Michael manage to create a good-sized pool, he embellished it with a stunning fountain and spa as well. There is very little maintenance required for the entire backyard, while its usability is pushed to the hilt. It also illustrates how much more a landscape designer can do for you than a pool contractor would—in this case, they all said "no" while Michael said "why not?"

Backyard Nirvana

The luxury of hydrotherapy has come home to the American backyard. Everyone who dreams of finishing the day with a dip in hot, turbulent spa waters may be pleased to find out how affordable this amenity has become. As we age, this prospect seems increasingly more attractive, and a spa is the perfect home improvement project no matter where you live.

The water-filled spa works hard for you. It is perfectly sized for a city townhouse or condominium yard. A portable unit is the solution for renters, and everyone will benefit from one that moves with you from house to house over time. The in-ground spa is a high-profile visual amenity when enhanced by fountains or waterfalls. It will provide you with both a focal point and an aid to relaxation and better health. Whether you are creating a high-end super-landscape or are on a tight budget, a new spa will make you feel better, enrich your life, and add a unique new living space to your yard.

FOR MAN IS NOT THE CREATURE AND PRODUCT OF MECHANISM; BUT, IN A FAR
TRUER SENSE, ITS CREATOR AND PRODUCER.

—THOMAS CARLYLE, *SIGN OF THE TIMES*, 1829

THE MECHANICS *of* WATER

EVERY WATER FEATURE, whether natural-appearing or rigidly

formal, must be well designed if it is to function properly. This is

the art of hydraulic engineering, rooted in the ancient world and

scaled down to our contemporary applications in the garden.

Throughout this book we have explored water feature design in

the garden and touched lightly on some of the mechanical

requirements unique to certain types of construction. Although

this chapter may prove redundant, a more direct reference will

help you find the technical information you need without wad-

ing through the rest of the book.

Moving Water with Pumps

All contemporary water features require a mechanical pump to recirculate the water. Two basic types of pumps are used today: the *submersible pump* and the *centrifugal turbine pump*. Each is located in a different part of the water feature.

The submersible pump is fully immersed in the water and usually sits in the bottom of the basin or pond. This makes it very quiet because the water buffers any operating noises. It must be connected to a power cord, and the hoses or pipes that feed the fountainhead are also routed down to the pump. Submersible pumps are corrosion resistant, lightweight, and affordable, with prices from $30 to $500, depending on the size.

In general, the residential-size submersible pump is limited to water features with an area no greater than about 100 square feet (about 30 square meters). Submersible pumps are rated according to how much water they will pump through over an hour's time. This rating is called *gallons per hour* (GPH), ranging between the minimum, 60 GPH, and the maximum, 5,000 GPH. Each pump motor will be rated by the Underwriters Laboratories (UL) according to its voltage—either a 115-volt or 230-volt motor.

The stainless steel and bronze pumps are the most reliable and long-lasting. They can be used in freshwater, salt water, or chlorinated water. These also withstand hot water up to 120° F (49° C). Other models are made of heavy-duty plastic, nontoxic plastic resin, cast aluminum, or epoxy encapsulated. Most portable unit fountains are equipped with the smaller plastic types.

Centrifugal turbine pumps are also known as *flooded-end pumps* and sit on dry land. The most common examples of these are swimming pool pumps. Centrifugal pumps are heavy-duty industrial products designed for continuous operation and constructed of corrosion-resistant cast bronze or heavy-duty plastic. These pumps are rated at either 120-volt or 240-volt and are used where large volumes of water are to be recirculated.

This type of pump, used in a residential setting, is available in these sizes rated by horsepower: ⅓ HP, ½ HP, ¾ HP, 1 HP, 1½ HP, or 3 HP. The pump is not attractive and must be hidden from view, yet close to the water feature. Its position is relative to the lowest pool in a multilevel fountain, rather than the fountainhead. The pump will require two pipes to recirculate the fountain, the inflow pipe, and the outgoing pipe.

FAR LEFT, This is an example of typical mechanical requirements for a pond and waterfall. The pump and filter are located in a warm climate, which allows them to sit exposed without frost damage. In colder regions, they would require a specially insulated housing or be located underground. AT LEFT, A controller such as this will turn the waterfall off and on at predetermined times. It may also control outdoor lighting so that the water feature is illuminated and flowing when you're most likely to be there to enjoy it.

The pump can be positioned farther away from the water feature, but this is a much more expensive choice for a number of reasons. The more distant the pump, the more high-pressure pipe must be installed. For each additional foot (about 30 cm) of pipe, there must be a slight increase in pump size to compensate for pressure reduction due to a factor known as *friction loss*. Friction loss can also be countered by larger-diameter pipe, which also raises installation costs dramatically.

Both types of pumps can be controlled by a switch or a remote control system, which turns it on or off and lets you control the rate of flow. You will be able to turn the volume to create a louder, more dramatic effect or a mere trickle, depending on your mood. These remote controls can be handheld and battery operated, or tied into a standard 120-volt electrical plug indoors. The remote allows you maximum flexibility to control the fountain without having to directly adjust it at the pump.

ABOVE LEFT, The orange gate valve handle stands out against the UV light–resistant black PVC pipe. The valve is used to shut off water to the pump and filter to allow repairs and cleaning. ABOVE RIGHT, This is a self-contained filter that functions whenever the water is flowing. It may require periodic cleaning or replacement of the filter media.

There are also new computer-controlled systems that allow a host of programmable effects. Such pumps should be installed on a dedicated circuit separate from other electrical service to the rest of the house. This separate circuit should also come with its own ground fault circuit interrupter for safety.

Piping Water

The recirculating pump can be connected by different types of pipe, and each one will have its own advantages and limitations.

Polyvinyl chloride (PVC) is noncorrosive, rigid, heavy-duty white plastic. Pressurized lines should be schedule 40 grade PVC. It is easy to install and as easy to repair as metal pipe. Because it experiences a low rate of friction loss due to the smoothness of its inside surfaces, you may use a smaller pump, too.

Its limitations include breakdown from exposure to extremes of temperature and ultraviolet light. All PVC should be buried, but if that is not possible it must be protected within a sleeve of opaque light-resistant material. The pipe and fittings are glued into place, which simplifies installation—but it is at these joints that they are most likely to fail. System vibration can place strain on the fittings, so all pipe must be securely anchored and supported against the inevitable water hammering as the pump turns on and off.

Copper pipe is also noncorrosive and much more structurally sound than PVC—particularly at fittings, which are soldered into place rather than glued. This pipe is moderately difficult to install. It can be cut and fitted to match any application, but flaring tools and soldering skills require experienced plumbing professionals. Copper pipe must be isolated from steel piping and fittings to avoid deterioration of the steel due to electrolysis. Copper is far more expensive in terms of both materials and labor than PVC, but piping applications larger than 3 inches (about 76 mm) in diameter often require a transition to metal pipe.

Steel pipe is also known as *galvanized pipe* because the raw metal is cloaked in a liquid sealer that reduces rust and corrosion. Steel pipe, unlike more adaptable plastic and copper, requires threaded joints, which makes it more difficult to install in custom applications and harder to repair. Therefore, smaller-diameter piping is typically copper, and piping over 3 inches (about 76 mm) in diameter is steel. This pipe should be galvanized or epoxy-lined to prevent rust formation on the inside, which will result in the staining of fountains. Galvanized pipe must not be directly attached to brass or bronze fittings, to avoid rapid corrosion.

POOL OR POND?
ACCORDING TO THE Uniform Building Code used across the United States, any water feature deeper than about 18 inches (about 46 cm) is considered a swimming pool. As such, it will require safety fencing and a building permit and subsequent inspection.

Water flow in all types of pipe is controlled by valves of varying design. Some merely open and shut, while others allow you to narrow the valve to any degree you wish to regulate the flow rate. The gate valve is very strong for secure on or off positions, and usually is made of brass. The others are variable-flow valves and may be constructed of PVC or brass. Depending on the design, they are called a *butterfly valve*, *globe valve*, or *ball valve*, and they may be electronically operated to allow you to control fountain flow behavior by remote.

Water In and Water Out

Larger fountains and waterfalls should be equipped with both a drain and an automatic fill device that ensures the water levels remain constant. The drain must be installed at the lowest point of the water feature, and is connected to a storm drain. The drain can be fitted with a stand pipe extended to the optimal surface level of the water, which allows it to double as an overflow. This is very important to prevent the pond from overfilling, either by accident or from heavy rainfall.

The automatic fill device is usually a niche-mounted float valve hidden out of sight somewhere around the rim of the pool. It acts like a toilet tank valve to automatically refill the fountain or pond when the water level falls below a certain level. When the water rises to the optimal level, it automatically shuts off. This automatic fill device eliminates the need to manually add water to the pool, which is important if you go on vacation. All water features suffer from evaporation, and unless the water is kept within its optimal range there can be performance problems, undesirable heating of the water, and algae bloom. This fill device must be installed with a backflow preventer to keep pond water from siphoning back into the domestic water supply.

Illumination

Lighting can be as important to a water feature as its overall design, because this is what contributes ethereal beauty after dark. Lighting makes water more visible and can illuminate key elements or enhance visual contrast between elements. Lighting can be submerged or positioned anywhere around the water feature for just the right effect.

Underwater lighting fixtures should be located about 2 inches (about 51 mm) below the water surface. They may be arranged to shine upward into the falling water, and the fixtures will vary according to the particular application.

Underwater floodlights are ideal for large-area coverage, such as multiple jets, spray rings, or cascades. The size of the light is determined by a light coverage ratio that compares height to width to determine the extent of its capabilities. A 1:1 floodlight will cover a relatively square area. It is best used for large-area effects, such as vertical bubblers, mushroom shapes, and waterfalls. Light coverage ratio 2:1, which is twice as tall as it is wide, is used for single-jet effects, including cascade, aerating, foam, and smooth-bore jets.

The use of colored lenses can enhance the effect of underwater lighting, but may also prove unsophisticated if not used properly. The addition of colored lenses does decrease the output, so to maintain the optimal level of illumination you must use higher-wattage fixtures, or more of them.

The following ratios are used as a guide to how many more fixtures you will need to achieve the same degree of illumination with a colored lens as you would with a clear lens:

- amber, 2 colored to 1 clear

- blue, 7 to 1

- green, 6 to 1

- red, 4 to 1

The best rule of thumb for determining how many lighting fixtures are needed to illuminate a water feature is to space them every 3 or 4 feet (about 1 m) for waterfalls, and use two fixtures per jet for fountains. For large fountains or ponds, consider additional overhead lighting as a supplement to underwater lighting.

In most situations a simple 12-volt lighting kit will do the job nicely and is easy for a homeowner to install without professional assistance. The kit includes outdoor wire, fixtures you can install anywhere along its length, and a transformer that plugs into any 110-volt outlet. If you plan lighting into your fountain project, remember that you will need two sockets: one for the fountain and a second for the transformer that controls the lights.

These lighting kits can be customized to create any effect you choose. They are classified as either ambient or decorative fixtures. *Ambient fixtures*, also known as *adjustable bullet lights*, are designed to be hidden under or behind plants and other objects so that all you see is the light, never the fixture itself. Adjustability is very important, and 12-volt systems allow you to not only adjust the angle of the bullet, but move the fixture as often as you wish to achieve optimal positioning. Remember that the plants around the fountain will grow larger over time, and to retain the same degree of illumination you will have to make periodic adjustments.

You may also buy submersible ambient lights that are dropped into the basin of the fountain and positioned to shine up to illuminate the falling water above. Though more expensive than dry lighting, these can magnify the presence and enhance the beauty of a fountain at night.

Decorative fixtures are designed to be seen both day and night. Better-quality 12-volt products made of bronze and glass double as attractive works of garden art in the daytime. One group mimic shapes of calla lily flowers in the graceful art nouveau style. A second very popular style reproduces the lovely geometric arts-and-crafts style using marbled or opaline stained glass.

ABOVE LEFT, Lighting set into the water to shine up on the most vital part of the feature is one of the most dramatic ways to make a fountain visible at night. ABOVE RIGHT, It is nearly impossible to install lighting after a fountain is designed and built. This uplight on the bottom of the pool requires a great deal of planning so that conduit and wiring are in place before the concrete is poured.

Other unique designer fixtures are used to complement various styles of fountains and landscapes. In the Southwestern or Santa Fe style, there is a preference for Mexican terra-cotta fixtures, or Spanish colonial glass and metal fixtures. Japanese gardens rely on the highly decorative pagoda lights that are both real garden art and functional path markers rooted in the tea ceremony. All of these decorative fixtures can be either 12-volt for less illumination ability, or hardwired as 110-volt luminaries for larger, more challenging sites.

Both fountain pumps and outdoor fountain light systems can be fitted with a simple automatic clock. It can be adjusted to turn one or both on at a predetermined time each day and turn it off later. This feature is particularly valuable when it comes to lighting, so that the fountain and its surroundings are automatically illuminated at dusk, then turned off at your bedtime.

A *photo cell* is an alternative to a time clock that is activated by sunlight or the lack of it. Fading light of sunset will turn the lights on until the sunrise triggers the cell to automatically turn them off again. The cell is not an efficient energy user because it leaves the lights on all night. If you only want the lights on in the evening, it is best to choose the time clock.

Be sure to inquire about all these features when you buy your fountain and light kits. It is always better to install everything at once rather than adding later on when your accessibility is hindered by mature plants. You can also ensure that all systems are compatible before you discover problems with installation. If you do not feel confident about installing lights and time clocks, consider hiring a landscape contractor.

Water Quality

Concerns for water quality are paramount in water features that contain plants and fish. Fish respiration and waste, uneaten food, and decaying leaves inevitably cause ammonia to build up in the water. When beneficial bacteria are present—which are often found in a biological filter—ammonia is reduced to nitrates, which can be taken up by plants and fish.

Filters are requisite in all but the smallest water feature if it is to contain plants or fish. They are operated by the circulating pump—the water is pushed through a filter media that acts like a strainer to collect leaves and other particulate matter. The filter must be checked regularly to ensure that it is functioning properly.

OPPOSITE, Lighting a landscape and a water feature requires many different fixtures that provide complete illumination without revealing the source of the light. Each of the fixtures is carefully located where it will be out of sight. This beautiful setting includes bullet spotlights on the arbor, spots in the planting around the fountain, and submerged lights in every tier of the fountainhead and its pool below.

Biological Filter

The most common type of filter for water gardens with plants and fish is called a *biological filter*. This filter requires no toxic chemicals, charcoal, or special media, just periodic cleaning. The filter is effective at reducing cumulative nitrogen and ammonia responsible for degrading water quality and stimulating algae bloom.

A biological filter has a very simple design. It is composed of a box or tube that sits submerged on the bottom of the pond. Water enters on one end and exits to the circulating pump on the other. The container is filled with a porous media, such as volcanic gravel or plastic mesh. The media is colonized with special bacteria that feed on ammonia and nitrogen, so as the water passes through the bacteria extract these toxins. The main problem with these filters is that the bacteria must be kept alive, and if the pump is turned off for any length of time the organisms starve and must be recolonized. Therefore, you must continuously run your pump.

External Filter

The *external filter* is composed of a box that sits on dry land near the water feature. Media can be volcanic rock or other products that function in the same way. The external filter does not remove nitrogen and ammonia as capably as a biological filter, but it is very effective for aerating the water and sifting out particulate matter.

Another kind of external filter that is more sophisticated uses fine silica sand as media, supported on a base of heavier sand and gravel. Trapped particles and nitrogen accumulate in the media, and are then flushed out by a process called *backwashing*. When selected valves are manipulated the flow is reversed, sending the accumulated debris into the drainage system while the clean water returns to the fountain. The frequency of backwashing relates to the size of the pond, its contents, and local climate.

Filters will require frequent cleaning. When too full or clogged, the filter may restrict the flow rate to your pump, and you will notice changes in the waterfall. Be sure you turn off the system before opening the filter to remove it for cleaning. If you use a submersible pump, check the intake screen and clean it to ensure maximum flow. A biological filter needs to have its media bed raked about once a month to remove accumulated debris. About twice a year the system should be vacuumed or backflushed to get rid of excess sludge or sediment.

Basic Maintenance

All water features require some major cleaning and maintenance. Those with plants and fish, which must strike a delicate balance, require more attention. Cleaning chlorinated fountains is a bit more rigorous, but you won't have the year-round chores of the water garden.

Chlorinated fountains and water features require cleaning periodically to remove any buildup of algae or minerals, which will discolor the surfaces. First, completely drain the water feature. To clean concrete or tile, use a solution of equal parts water and muratic acid. Be sure to wear rubber gloves and eye gear, and use a wire brush to scour the surfaces clean. Rinse the pool completely and let it dry empty for about two days. Then rinse a second time and allow the pool to dry overnight. In the morning, fill with water and adjust the pool's chemical balance.

If you have a spray fountainhead, clean the orifices with a needle to remove any mineral buildup that may restrict the flow rate. If you have problem water, you may have to do this as often as every 30 to 60 days to keep it flowing at optimal rates.

You should expect to drain and thoroughly clean a water garden at least once each year. This is in addition to regular ongoing debris and algae control. To clean a water garden pool, first remove all plants and fish, then drain it entirely. Remove sediment and debris accumulation without damaging the plastic liner or the sometimes brittle concrete shell. It is important not to scrub or heavily scrape the shell, because this is where the naturally occurring beneficial bacteria resides. Thoroughly inspect for any sign of damage or potential leaks, then refill and replace plants and fish.

It's What You Don't See That Counts

Although we are concerned with aesthetics, the beauty of any water feature is negated if it does not function as intended. Even a small project can cost thousands of dollars once surroundings and plants are factored in. With that kind of investment, no one can afford to overlook the mechanical requirements needed to ensure that it remains a beautiful, satisfying amenity for many years to come.

With their many factors, sizeable projects should be managed by an experienced contractor to avoid the common pitfalls of do-it-yourself projects gone awry. Plumbing is essential to water circulation in both the fill and the drain. The filter keeps the water feature from turning green with uncontrolled algae bloom. Pumps are vital to aeration and the animation of the overall design. Lighting dictates whether it will be a glowing focal point after dark or a black corner of the garden. Building right the first time means your beautiful water feature won't turn into a dry planter.

RESOURCES: FOUNTAIN AND EQUIPMENT SUPPLIERS

The following resources are not the only ones available today, but they do represent the major companies in the upscale water feature marketplace. There are many others that serve only certain states and regions. It is always better to work with a local company if one is nearby, because they will be able to help you choose fountains and equipment compatible with your regional climate conditions. The demands of winter in Nebraska will be very different from those in Louisiana, and you must choose products that you can count on without inordinate amounts of maintenance. Beautiful artwork, such as cast metal antique fountain replicas, are such special products that they may only be available from a few sources.

Aardvark Antiques
475 Thames Street, Newport, RI 02840
(401) 849-7233
www.aardvarkantiques.com
Global supplier of antique and re-created architectural fountain elements

Arcadia Ceramics, Inc.
369 Meyer Circle, Corona, CA 91719
(800) 754-9312
E-mail: foun437@aol.com
Quality ceramic wall fountains

The Brass Baron
10151 Pacific Mesa Boulevard, San Diego, CA 92121
(800) 536-0987
www.brassbaron.com
Largest selection of brass fountains and statuary in the United States

Country Flair Tile
Kent Green Shopping Village
Kent, CT 06757
(860) 927-3178
www.homeandgardendecor.com
Hand-carved fountains and millstones with brass spigots

Festive Fountains
61 St. Andrews Drive, Rochester, NY 14626
(716) 225-0083
Suppliers of water display equipment, cascades, waterfalls, fountains, and electronic control devices

Florentine Craftsmen, Inc.
46-24 28th Street, Box TB, Long Island City, NY 11101
(718) 937-7632
www.florentinecraftsmen.com
The finest in garden ornaments, statuary, and fountains, handcrafted in lead, iron, aluminum, bronze, and stone

The Garden Gallery
3020 'H' Street, Sacramento, CA 95816
(916) 444-1844
Bronze fountains and accessories

Giannini
344 Victory Avenue South, San Francisco, CA 94080
(650) 873-4493
Concrete fountains and garden accessories

Haddonstone USA Ltd.
201 Heller Place, Bellmawr, NJ 08031
(856) 931-7011
www.haddonstone.com
Cast-reconstructed freestanding, self-contained, and wall fountains with plumbing and pool liner accessories

Kenneth Lynch & Sons
84 Danbury Road, P.O. Box 488, Wilton, CT 06897-0488
(203) 762-8363
www.klynchandsons.com
Architectural ornamental metal and stone fountains

Long Island Fountain Supply Co.
10-2 Drew Court, Ronkonkoma, NY 11779
(631) 467-5295
www.lifountain.com/new
Supplier of fountain nozzles, pumps, lighting, controls, and prefabricated self-contained fountains

Oase Pumps, Inc.
17322 Murphy Avenue, Irvine, CA 92614
(800) 365-3880
www.oasepumps.com
Manufacturer of decorative water feature equipment, pumps, filtration, lighting, and specialty nozzles

Otterbine Barebo, Inc.
3840 Main Road East, Emmaus, PA 18049
(800) 237-8837
www.otterbine.com
Manufacturer of fountains, water-quality management products, underwater lighting, ozone generation systems, and biological water treatments

Robinson Iron
P.O. Box 1119, Alexander City, AL 35011-1119
(205) 329-8486
Large selection of cast iron products, including sculpture, fountains, and fencing

Stone Forest
P.O. Box 2840, Santa Fe, NM 87504
(888) 682-2987
www.stoneforest.com
Supplier of hand-carved stone fountains and Japanese garden elements

Stone Legends
301 Pleasant Drive, Dallas, TX 75217
(800) 398-1199
www.stonelegends.com
Cast stone fountains and custom casting

Tetra Pond Supplies
301 Commerce Street, Blacksbury, VA 24060-6671
(703) 951-5400
Everything for ponds and water gardens, except the plants

Van Ness Water Gardens
2460 North Euclid Avenue, Upland, CA 91784-1199
(800) 205-2425
www.vnwg.com
Specializing in ecosystems featuring most products and plants for small ponds to large lakes